D1436156

The Barbary Slaves

The Barbary Slaves

STEPHEN CLISSOLD

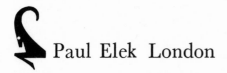 Paul Elek London

First published 1977 by
ELEK BOOKS LIMITED
54–58 Caledonian Road
London N1 9RN

ISBN 0 236 40084 3

Printed in Great Britain by
Unwin Brothers Limited
The Gresham Press, Old Woking, Surrey
A member of the Staples Printing Group

Contents

Plates

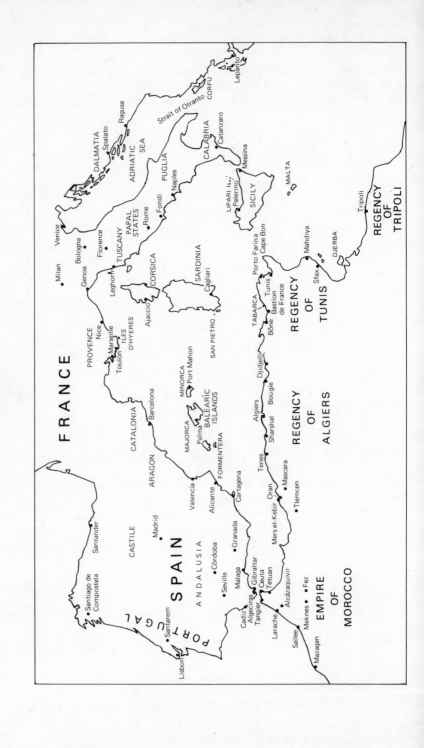

I

Into Bondage

One morning in 1593 a group of frightened and bewildered men were put ashore on a small island near the Gulf of Naples. Their captors sat at ease not far off, smoking and chatting round a fire whilst they waited for the slaves to take fresh water aboard their galley and for the strong winds which were hindering their journey back to Barbary to abate. Most of the captives were Italian fishermen, but one, though half naked like his companions, appeared to be a Spaniard distinguished by his breeding and natural air of authority. Suddenly one of the corsairs seated round the fire drew from it a piece of iron which he had been heating and walked over to the captives. Motioning to the Spaniard to stretch out his leg, he drew the red-hot metal across the sole of his foot. He then returned to the fire to reheat the iron and repeated the operation, tracing a second line at right angles to the first so as to make the sign of the cross. The galley-slaves, grimly familiar with the ways of their masters, whispered that the branding was meant to ensure a prosperous voyage and safe return to their base, but should things turn out otherwise, the corsairs would avenge themselves by having their captive burned alive. 'On hearing this,' the Spaniard wryly recalled, 'I offered up a fervent prayer that it might be even as they desired, for I feared the flames.'[1] That a Christian should be forced to trample the symbol of his faith under foot and pray for the success of the infidels was a bitter reminder that his world had been suddenly and disastrously turned upside down.

The Spaniard was a priest called Father Jerónimo Gracián. An outstanding and controversial figure amongst his contemporaries, he had once been a close friend of St Teresa of Avila and a leader of her reform movement. Ousted after the saint's death by his enemies in the Carmelite Order, he had sought rehabilitation—with little success—in Rome and been captured on his way back. The corsairs stripped him of his habit, rifled his few possessions, and cleaned their muskets with the manuscript which he had just completed on Mystical Theology. Sailing into the Gulf of Naples, the corsairs then sacked a church and rounded up more Christians before returning, laden with booty and nearly two hundred captives, to Tunis, where we shall meet with Father Gracián again. It was only a minor episode in the series of incessant raids against the shipping and coasts of Christendom which the Barbary corsairs had been launching since the beginning of the century.

A couple of decades later we find the corsairs venturing out into the Atlantic. Keeping their light oar-propelled craft for use in the Mediterranean, they learned to sail the 'round-ships' which enabled them greatly to increase the radius of their operations. Emanuel d'Aranda, a young Fleming returning home from Spain with three of his countrymen on board an English merchantman in August 1640, has described what was liable to happen. As she approached the English Channel, the merchantman found herself pursued by three unidentified sail. When they came within hailing distance, a sailor standing on the poop of the foremost ship unfurled a green, crescent-spangled banner and called out to them in the name of Algiers to surrender. The corsairs swarmed on deck and d'Aranda found himself confronted by a soldier in Turkish dress who addressed him in Flemish but turned out to be a renegade Englishman. 'Patience, brother, 'tis the fortune of war,' his captor exclaimed as he stripped him. 'My turn today, yours tomorrow!' Passengers and crew were rounded up and transferred to the pirate ships whilst a prize crew was put aboard the merchantman. 'I seemed like one in a dream, and the figures moving around me strange ghosts inspiring fear, wonder and curiosity. They wore strange clothes, spoke strange tongues—Turkish, Arabic, *lingua franca*, as well as Spanish, French, Flemish and English—bore strange arms, and made strange gesticulations when they prayed.'² Such were the captives' sensations of fascinated horror and foreboding as they were carried off to Algiers and slavery.

For nearly two centuries much the same tactics continued to be used to harass the ships of Christendom. North to Ireland and even to Iceland, south to the Canaries, westwards far out into the Atlantic the corsairs roved in search of unsuspecting victims. One morning in October 1793 the American brig *Polly*, bound for Cadiz, was approaching Cape St Vincent when the look-out caught sight of a ship flying the English flag and bearing down upon her. A man dressed in European fashion could be seen on deck, and when they got near enough, he hailed the *Polly* in English. John Foss, one of the American seamen, recalled the sudden change of scene.

> We saw several men jump upon her poop to haul aft the main sheet, and saw by their dress and long beards they were Moors or Algerians. We heard a most terrible shouting, clapping of hands, huzzaing, etcetera, and saw a great number of men rise with their heads above the gunnel, dressed in the Turkish habit like those we saw on the poop. They immediately hoisted out a large launch, and about a hundred of the pirates jumped on board, all armed, some with scimitars and pistols, others with pikes, spears, lances and knives. As soon as they came on board our vessel, they made signs for us all to go forward, assuring us in several languages that if we did not obey their commands, they would immediately massacre us all. They then went below in the cabin, steerage, and every place where they could get below deck and broke open all the trunks and chests that were on board, and plundered all our bedding, clothing, books, charts, quadrants and every movable article that did not consist of the cargo or furniture. They then came on deck, like a pack of ravenous wolves, and stripped the clothes off our backs, all except a piece of shirt and pair of drawers (myself being left with no shirt at all).

The next day, an old Turk approached Foss, and 'with an air of kindness', bestowed on him a tattered sleeveless shirt —the only time, in the years of captivity about to begin in Barbary, that 'he was to find a Moslem in whom a spark of humanity was to be seen'.[3]

It was not only of clothes and material possessions that a captive would find himself stripped. The day a man becomes a slave, Homer says, he loses half his soul. He becomes a mere thing, to be kept or sold at his captor's whim, valued only for the muscle which may ply his master's oar or till his fields. This sudden deprivation of human status has been a fate to which men were liable, especially in the pirate-infested Mediterranean, from time immemorial. What may surprise us is its persistence and institutionalization during the very period when Europe's technological superiority was leading to worldwide expansion and ascendancy. Yet we have seen today how the guerrilla or terrorist can impose his will by gaining tactical superiority over a far more powerful enemy through the same weapons of surprise, holding to ransom, blackmail and the extortion of protection money which were the corsair's stock-in-trade. The North African slave-prison was as grim a feature of those times as the labour- or concentration-camp has been of ours. Barbary was Christendom's Gulag Archipelago.

Many, perhaps most, of those taken died in captivity. Some came to terms as best they could with their servile lot in the alien world of Islam, and might have little cause for complaint if lucky enough to find a good master. Release from the Barbary Gulag could only be expected in one of two ways; through apostasy or ransom. The Christian who abjured his faith did not automatically cease to be a slave. But he did gain immunity from the harshest form of slavery, since only Christians might be employed at the galley-oar; he could generally hope for better treatment and eventual manumission, for a pious master would arrange for his Moslem slaves to be freed on his death, if not before. Pressure to apostatize was commonly applied only against young men who had the makings of good soldiers and corsairs, distinguished captives whose conversion would be a resounding propaganda coup, or women wanted for the harem, whilst children would simply be brought up as young Moslems. Though many succumbed to such pressure and to despair of ever returning to their native land, there were others who actively sought a change of religion as a means of bettering themselves. Whilst Catholics struggled against Protestants in Europe, a constant stream of adventurers made their way to the Barbary coast in order to enlist under the banner of Islam. The skills brought by these deserters from Christendom and by those captives who, freely or under compulsion, offered similar services, constituted a form of technical assistance bestowed by Christian Europe on its traditional foe. They cast and manned the cannon, built and sailed the ships, and performed many other essential tasks which helped the corsairs to ply their trade.

For the captive determined to remain true to his faith—apart from the handful who managed to escape or were freed after a Christian victory—ransom offered the one hope of regaining freedom. The ransoming of prisoners had been a common practice in mediaeval Europe and during the Crusades. Feudal tenants had the obligation of contributing towards their lord's ransom, and a whole realm—as Richard Lionheart's subjects knew to their cost—might be taxed for the same purpose. Burghers might sell up their possessions in order to raise an indemnity which would save their city from sack. But hope of securing ransom payments, which may at first have mitigated the ferocity of war, became itself a spur to aggression. The corsairs came to look upon the seizure of booty and captives not as the by-product of a war waged for religious or political ends, but as the end in itself. Their states were organized and geared for this over-riding purpose. They drew their revenues largely from the sale of prizes and captives, and from the tribute and 'presents' which purchased temporary immunity. Their fleets, though participating—often reluctantly—in the Grand Signior's naval operations, were adapted principally for the pursuit and capture of foreign merchantmen and for slave-raids into Christian territory. Christian slaves powered the galleys, furnished domestic labour and skilled craftsmen and cultivated the gardens and orchards around Algiers, the chief corsair city. Such trade as developed was inextricably interwoven with piracy, for goods plundered from prizes or—like gunpowder and other war material—received as tribute, formed an important part of their imports. The whole economy was oiled, and the key janissary corps largely paid, with the revenue received from ransoms and indemnities.

In the Christian countries most affected, special machinery was set up for the ransoming of captives. Pioneers in the art of fund-raising, the Trinitarians in France, the Mercedarians in Spain, and other organizations in Italy and even in northern Europe sent missions to Barbary and cooperated with Jewish and other merchant intermediaries to redeem the captives and meet the corsairs' insatiable demands. Later, the European governments themselves, through special embassies or resident consuls, entered the business, and also attempted to negotiate treaties safeguarding their own ships and nationals. In this way the countries of Christendom, either through impotence or a cynical calculation that they stood to suffer less than their political and commercial rivals, came to acquiesce in the continued depredations of the corsairs. The latter, finding that blackmail yielded rich rewards, continued to take ever more captives and to raise their demands. They saw themselves not as pirates but as corsairs operating by virtue of time-honoured custom—*usanza del mare*—and subject only to a code of their own regulating the share-out of the booty amongst themselves. A vast web of complicity thus came to be woven about their activities, linking together the marauders who believed that Providence had conferred upon them this special licence to plunder and enslave, the charitable organizations and sometimes unscrupulous intermediaries, and the European states which occasionally sought to suppress, but more often merely to divert against their rivals, this anomalous survival of the ancient struggle between Cross and Crescent.

2

Moors and Christians

In 711 the first Moslem detachments crossed the Straits from North Africa to begin the rapid conquest of the Iberian peninsula. A large part of the Christian population accepted the faith of their conquerors and gradually merged with them in the new Islamic state of al-Andalus. Others lived on as tolerated but despised Christian communities under Moslem rule. A handful of intransigents maintained a precarious independence in the northern mountains and gradually fought their way southwards in the long and intermittent process of the Reconquest. The Moslems' *Jihad* or Holy War was answered by the Christians' Crusade. Though the regaining of the whole peninsula for the Cross remained the latter's grand objective, the Christians were no less ready than the Moslem invaders had been to exploit their opportunities for personal gain. Incursions into enemy territory were often undertaken less with a view to permanent occupation than for the seizure of booty and captives. The latter were commonly reduced to slavery.

Both the rival faiths accepted slavery as an institution, though it lasted longer, and loomed larger, in Moslem society than in Christian Europe. War against the infidels was regarded by Islam as a legitimate source of slaves. But once the sword was sheathed, the freeing of captives, or their ransoming, was enjoined as a pious work. One saying attributed to the Prophet exhorts his followers to 'give them such food as you eat yourselves, clothe them in such garments as you wear yourselves, and burden them not with labours too heavy for them. Those of them you like, keep; those you dislike, sell; but do not torment God's creatures'.[1] Practice, however, often fell as far short of these humane precepts amongst the Moslems as it did amongst the Christians.

The Iberian peninsula was the borderland where the clash between the Christian and Islamic worlds was longest and

fiercest. Immense numbers of captives were taken by warlike
and ruthless princes such as al-Mansūr (Almanzor, 938–1002);
the chronicles speak of 30,000 in one campaign alone against
the Kingdom of León. After the great Christian defeat at
Alarcos (1195), 5,000 Christians were exchanged against an
equal number of Moslems, and so many remained that they
were sold off at the derisory price of one dirham—a small silver
coin—a head. Captives were commonly employed on public
works, such as the construction of the great mosque at Córdoba,
set to work on the land, or disposed of at slave auctions. Some
were enrolled in the Emir of Córdoba's personal body-guard—a
precedent already set by the rulers of Byzantium and Baghdad.

Al-Andalus became an important centre for the Moslem
slave-trade. Sudanese and 'Slavonians'—captives made from
the warlike Slav tribes on the eastern confines of Europe and
purchased through dealers—were imported for the domestic
market. Christians were acquired not only for labour in the
peninsula but for export to other Moslem countries. Córdoba
and other principal cities had their *ma'rid* where the human
merchandise was examined along lines which the slave-
dealers were to follow, though with less sophistication, in the
slave-marts of Barbary. Women were generally prized more
highly than men, and were classified in two categories; the
'distinguished' or first class (*murtafa'at*) and the 'common'.
They were examined, before being offered for sale, by a female
inspector (*amina*) who kept a meticulous record, which was then
specified in the purchase contract, of the physical attractions
(*nu'ut*) and defects (*uyub*) of each human chattel. Handbooks
listing these good and bad qualities were specially composed to
facilitate this delicate task.[2]

The wealthier captives on either side might hope to buy their
way out of misfortune through the offer of a ransom. The
Moslems seem to have taken the lead in devising machinery
to this end. In Córdoba an organization of professional ransomers (*fakkak*) was in existence from the tenth century, and
perhaps earlier; their activities must have become widespread
and familiar throughout Christian Spain, since they have given
the term *alfaqueque* to the Spanish language. These intermediaries offered their services to Moslem families whose
members had fallen into Christian hands. Contracts were

drawn up authorizing the *alfaqueque*, in return for a specified sum, to cross into Christian territory and negotiate the ransom and return of the captive. The contract also laid down what was to be done in the event of the captive having died or escaped. Whether these *alfaqueques* were always Moslems, or whether the Jewish merchant-negotiators later so prominent in the ransom business had begun to play a part, is not clear.

Until the thirteenth century, when the redemption of captives came to be arranged more and more through large-scale exchanges negotiated by treaty, ransoming seems to have been conducted chiefly through this form of private enterprise. To free or ransom a captive, as we have noted, was held to be a work of piety; legacies were made for this purpose and collections taken in the mosques. Arab historians record cases, such as that of a pious Moslem of Huesca who died in A.D. 919 after ransoming no less than 150 captives at his own expense.[3] Exceptionally, a captive might apparently be given conditional freedom so that he could collect his own ransom money. A *sufi* called Abu Yafur, taken and well treated by the Christians, was allowed to return home in order to collect his 500-dinar ransom. This he proceeded to do by begging trifling alms from as many good Moslems as possible so that all should have an opportunity of acquiring merit through the exercise of charity.[4]

More often than not, it is to be feared, the prospect of ransom excited anything but virtuous reactions. That most infamous of characters in the sombre drama of slavery—the informer who seeks to curry favour by betraying others into captivity—makes an early appearance. In A.D. 987 the Moors attacked Coimbra and carried off most of the inhabitants. Some managed to hide in the forests but were lured into an ambush by one of their number, and Almanzor's lieutenant had the satisfaction of selling them all profitably at the Santarem slave-market.[5] Families who had the misfortune to live on either side of the shifting frontier between Moorish and Christian areas were most exposed to the danger of being sold into slavery. The Moslem rulers, though not always able to protect their subjects in such outposts, were not unmindful of their plight. We read of al-Hakam I presenting his Moorish subjects living on the frontiers of his kingdom with a number of

Christian captives whom they could barter against any of their own number who might fall into enemy hands.

What, during those early centuries of the Reconquest, were the Christians of Spain doing on behalf of their captive co-religionists? Measures must have been taken, perhaps through the Moslem *alfaqueques* or some counterparts from the Christian areas, for the payment of ransom, since we find frequent testamentary behests in land or cash for this charitable purpose. Kings and other notables, not always remarkable for piety during their lifetime, sought to make amends by princely legacies of this sort; Peter the Cruel (d. 1369) bequeathed 100,000 golden doubloons for the redemption of a thousand captives. Towns and guilds, as well as close relatives, began to interest themselves in the captives' fate. Doubtless too there were initiatives, before any institutional machinery was set up by the Church, on the part of individual priests and friars. Certain saints seem, from an early date, to have been invoked as the special patrons of captive Christians, and their shrines to have been frequented by pilgrims seeking the saint's intercession or returning thanks to him for their own deliverance. By the twelfth century, the tomb of St James at Santiago de Compostela, spared by Almanzor when his troops razed the surrounding town to the ground in 997, had become the holiest place in Christian Spain. The Knights of Santiago, founded to protect the route to the shrine and to wage war against the enemies of the faith, extended their concern to Christians who fell into Moorish hands, whilst along the pilgrim road itself, we know of at least one great monastery— St Domingo de Silos—which was much visited by pilgrims attracted by the frequent and reputedly miraculous intervention of its patron or desiring to return thanks for their own safe return from captivity.

Towards the end of the thirteenth century a Benedictine monk from Silos called Pero Marín compiled an account in the vernacular of sixty-eight miracles ascribed to St Domingo for the deliverance of Christian captives.[6] The latter's stories, as related in the monk's *Miráculos romanizados*, afford vivid insights into the way in which ordinary men and women might suddenly find themselves kidnapped, the labour and sufferings they endured in captivity, and their faith in the supernatural intervention which restored them to freedom. Some were soldiers, captured in the course of more or less regular operations, but many were civilians seized by pirates or raiding parties. A merchant sailing from Santander with a cargo of cloth and wine for the Moslem port of Algeciras, supposedly then at peace with the Christians, had nevertheless been made prisoner by Moorish corsairs. Men had been carried off whilst tending their cattle, and women whilst working in the vineyards. The victims were sold off by their captors, sometimes changing hands at a profit. The prices they fetched varied enormously. We learn from the *Miráculos romanizados* that a captive passed from one master to another at 13, 15, 20 and finally 25 maravedís, and even grew indignant that so low a value was set on his person, since the current price for a donkey was only 20 maravedís; presumably he had already resolved to regain his liberty through escaping rather than awaiting ransom.

The first concern of all captives, whether Moslem or Christian, was to try to convince their captors of their lowly condition so that the ransom demanded of them might be kept low. The more valuable prisoners were often kept chained in pits or dungeons known as *mazmorras* pending the negotiating of a ransom. This was sometimes fixed at so much in cash and the balance in kind—a measure of oil or salt, a load of figs, or a bale of cloth. Arms, horses, or anything which might increase the war potential of the enemy would not be handed over as part of a ransom. The common run of captives were set to work in the fields, digging, ploughing and looking after the animals, or made to grind corn or turn the heavy *noria* wheels drawing the water with which Moorish farmers irrigated their land. Even when toiling they were kept fettered and under guard, and many complained of being ill-treated or starved. One wretch was made to grind grain with an iron gag over his mouth to prevent him satisfying his hunger. But doleful as the plight of such captives might be, it was nothing compared to the lot of those who were sold into slavery overseas, for escape then became virtually impossible and all hope of regaining freedom vanished. The prospect of being transported to Africa was thus dreaded more than anything else. We read of a certain García calling out in his anguish to St Domingo whilst he was being

taken to Ceuta. Immediately a storm blew up and he heard
the saint bidding him return to a Christian land. Then, 'how
it was he could not tell, but when dawn came he found himself
on shore near Lucena', and he was able to make good his
escape.

Other captives related similar experiences. Many vowed that
they had seen a dazzling light and heard the saint's voice, either
in a dream or when they were wide awake, bidding them
escape. Sometimes they would find beside them a knife or file
with which they could free themselves, or their fetters would
simply fall from them. Or they might make off regardless of
their chains, which they would later hang up as ex-votos in the
saint's shrine. If they escaped by night, the saint would light
them with his radiance; if by day, he would keep the Moors
from seeing them and the dogs from barking. At times he would
encourage them to feats of daring and endurance, even of
homicidal violence. One captive found a rowing boat in which
St Domingo sustained him for two days and nights without
food until he reached a Christian shore. Domingo Muñoz,
kept a captive in Almería, was sent with another slave to work
in a stone quarry. Suddenly he heard a voice exhorting him:
'Do what you have in your heart to do, and return to a
Christian land!' He looked about him but saw no one, except
his master who was drawing water at the *noria*. The two slaves
set upon him with their tools and threw his corpse into the
well. St Domingo then enabled the fugitives to reach safety.
Other captives described similar escapes. One had the satisfaction of seeing his master enslaved by the Christian raiding
party which gave him his own liberty.

By the end of the twelfth century the first institution
specifically concerned with the plight of Christian captives had
come into being. The Order of the Most Holy Trinity for the
Ransom of Captives received papal sanction in 1198 and began
its activities the following year with a venture to Morocco—
the first of many missions of mercy which were to continue
intermittently for more than five and a half centuries. The
origins of the Order are shrouded in legend. The latter relates
that its founder was John de Matha, a son of a Provençal
noble, and that he was vouchsafed a vision whilst saying his
first mass in Paris. John beheld a white-robed angel, with a red

and blue cross on his breast, and a slave standing on either side of him, one of them a turbaned Turk. The colours symbolized the Trinity; white for God the Father, blue for the bruised body of the crucified Son, and red for the flame of the Holy Spirit. The angel had his hands crossed in a gesture which indicated that the slaves were to be exchanged. John told his superiors of the vision and went to muse on its full meaning in the solitude of the forests near Meaux. There he encountered a hermit called Felix, and together the two men devoted themselves to a life of contemplation. One day they saw a stag come down to drink at a spring; on his head, instead of antlers, he carried a blue and red cross, like that which John had seen in his vision. John and Felix went to report this new wonder to the Bishop of Paris and to two saintly Abbots who advised them to bear their tidings to the Pope. Innocent III, who had already sponsored the Dominicans and the Franciscans, was at first in no mind to authorize any new Order. But when celebrating mass, he too was granted the self-same vision. Thus the Order of the Trinity won papal authorization; John became its first head, whilst Felix acted as its adviser. A white tunic emblazoned with a distinctive cross—a red upright and a blue cross-bar—was adopted as the habit, and the first monastery was established at the spot, now appropriately known as Cerf-froid or Cerfroy, where the stag had come to drink at the cool spring. One third of the Order's revenues was pledged for the work of ransom.

Whether St John de Matha was inspired to embark on his charitable work through such symbolic visions, and whether or not he enjoyed the concourse of the saintly Felix of Valois (whose very existence is doubted by some scholars), it is certain that Innocent III believed that Christendom would benefit from a new institution designed to care for and redeem the captives which the enemies of the faith continued to take in growing numbers. Though the mother-house of the new Order remained at Cerfroy, its executive headquarters, where the Grand Minister resided, operated from St Maturin's in Paris. The Trinitarians thus also came to be known as 'Maturins', or as 'Donkey-brothers', on account of their predilection for that humble mode of transport. King Louis IX (the saint), who himself experienced the bitterness of captivity at the hands of the Saracens, favoured the Order, taking its members with him on the Crusades, and selecting his chaplains from amongst their number. By the end of the thirteenth century, a hundred or so Trinitarian houses had been established from Canterbury to Bethlehem, many of them in Spain, in the domains of the king of Aragon.

Of the missions of redemption undertaken by the Order in the early years of its existence, we know regrettably little. We learn from the letter which Innocent III addressed in Latin to the king of Morocco, commending the ransomers in the assurance that their labours would be of mutual benefit to captors and captives, that they were two in number. One of them may well have been John de Matha himself. They are said to have been well received by the king and to have returned, after a month in Morocco, with 186 Christian slaves freed by purchase or through exchange.[7] On his way back from a similarly fruitful journey to Tunis St John is credited with a singular miracle. Some Moslems, angered at the effrontery of the Christian, sailed after him, but when they overtook him contented themselves with destroying the sails of his ship instead of killing him. Left to the mercy of wind and tide, the saint spread his cloak upon the mast and prayed earnestly to the Trinity, and he was in due course wafted to a friendly shore. Other journeys are attributed to St John, both to Tunis and to Spain, where he is said to have ransomed many captives in Valencia and to have made a number of foundations. Little as we know of him with certainty, and due allowance made for the embroideries of hagiography, John de Matha must have been a man of exceptional vision, enterprise and courage, whose example continued to inspire a series of heroic successors down the ages.

The Order of Our Lady of Mercy was established a few years after that of the Holy Trinity, probably in 1218; the exact date, like much else about its origins, is a matter of dispute. Its founder, St Peter Nolasco, was a Frenchman who left his birthplace near Carcassonne, probably to escape the Albigensian troubles, and settled in Aragon. There he became associated with King Jaime I, possibly as his tutor, and may have accompanied that monarch in his conquest of Valencia from the Moors. The statutes which he drew up for his new Order, with the help of the great theologian, administrator and king's councillor St Raymond of Peñafort, contained one notable innovation. In addition to the usual vows of chastity, poverty and obedience, its members were to take a fourth—to surrender themselves, if need be, as hostages to the Moors and to remain in captivity pending the payment of the ransoms demanded. In the eight decades which elapsed between the foundation of the Order and the end of the century, the Mercedarians are said to have carried out about seventy missions to the Moslem territories of Spain and North Africa, seventeen of them losing their lives in the process and another eight remaining as hostages.[8] The helpers whom St Peter gathered round him must have been a remarkable and heroic band of men, though their exploits are known to us only through the magnifying glass of legend: St Raymond Non-natus (later revered as the patron saint of midwives, since he had been taken from his mother's womb after she had died in childbirth), whom his captors had to silence with an iron gag to prevent him preaching the gospel; St Peter Armengol, a converted bandit, who would have ended his life on the gallows had not Our Lady herself miraculously suspended his body in the air; and an English knight called Serapio (*será pío*—'he shall be pious', according to the dubious etymology of the hagiographers), who went crusading with Richard Lionheart, founded Mercedarian monasteries in England, Scotland and Ireland, and suffered martyrdom at the stake in Barbary.

The Christian Reconquest of Spain was held up by new waves of Moslem invaders from Morocco and by internecine quarrels amongst the Christian princes. By the last quarter of the fifteenth century, however, only the Kingdom of Granada was holding out against the armies of the Catholic Monarchs, Ferdinand and Isabella. One by one, the cities recovered by the Christians were forced to give up their quota of slaves. When Ronda fell, 400 liberated slaves were received in audience by the Monarchs to render thanks before hanging up their fetters as ex-votos in the churches. In Málaga, the beleaguered Moslems tried to get improved terms by threatening to hang their Christian prisoners from the battlements. The Catholic Monarchs replied that they would then put every Moslem man, woman and child to the sword, and punished the city for its defiance by enslaving the entire population, though in fact the Christian captives were handed over unharmed. One-third of Málaga's inhabitants were sent to Africa to be exchanged for an equal number of Christian slaves there; one-third went to the state to defray the expenses of the campaign; and the remaining third were shared out as booty amongst the victorious army. Fifty Moorish maidens were sent as gifts to the queen of Naples, thirty to the queen of Portugal, and others to the ladies of the Court, whilst the Pope received one hundred warriors who were incorporated into his guard and in time—so we are assured—turned into very good Christians.

The harsh fate meted out to the Malagueños was probably intended to intimidate the inhabitants of Granada into accepting the far more generous terms which the Catholic Monarchs were prepared to extend to them. Any Moslems who wished were offered a passage to Africa, whilst those who chose to remain under Spanish suzerainty were promised the full enjoyment of their religious and legal rights. All Christian slaves were to be unconditionally released, but if a Moslem could prove that he had sold his slaves into Barbary before the signature of the Capitulations, restitution would not be required of him. All ships conveying the exiles and their belongings would however be carefully searched to make sure that no slaves were being smuggled away on board.[9]

The capture of Granada closed the long chapter of the Christian Reconquest of the peninsula. But it did not signal the definitive triumph of the Cross over the Crescent in the western Mediterranean, nor guarantee individual Christians against being enslaved by the enemies of their faith. It heralded rather a new stage of Moslem militancy. For more than three centuries, thousands of men, women and children from the Mediterranean lands—and from remoter parts of Christendom as well—were to taste the harsh experience of Barbary slavery.

3

The Rise of the Barbary States

'Barbary' took its name from its indigenous Berber inhabitants, tribes of pastoralists and mountain-dwellers, and 'barbarians' in the eyes of its more sophisticated townsfolk and conquerors— Phoenicians, Romans, Byzantines. The Arabs who implanted their rule and their religion in the seventh century gave it the more romantic name of Djezira al Maghrib—the Island in the West. This vast territory stretching between Egypt and the Atlantic has indeed something of the character of an island, or rather of an archipelago, for the towns and cultivated areas are often separated from each other by wide tracts of wilderness. Bounded in the north by the Mediterranean, in the south by the more indeterminate borders of the Sahara, and flanked by the lofty ranges of the Atlas Mountains, it turns its back on the continent and faces towards the inland sea; but it is a Mediterranean land with a difference. Ancient caravan routes, with their precious loads of gold and black slaves, linked it with the East and the African lands to the south. Arab conquerors irrupted into it, and later, zealots from the tribes of the interior. Twice, first under the Almoravids and then under the Almohads, a centre of Moslem power was established which for a time dominated the whole Maghrib and reanimated Moslem agression in Spain. Morocco, the seat of this imperial power, by its inaccessibility and distinctive character as an Atlantic as well as a Mediterranean country, is not strictly to be reckoned amongst the Barbary states, but its history has been so intertwined with theirs that it was commonly so regarded and may here be considered as such. Tunis, Tripoli and Algiers will concern us still more closely in their role of corsair and slave-owning states.

Nature seemed to have shaped the Barbary coast specially for this role. From Tripoli in the east to the Straits of Gibraltar in the west—and beyond, if we include the pirate lair from which the 'Sallee Rovers' pounced on Atlantic shipping—it abounded in sheltered anchorages which ranged from the capacious harbours of Tunis or Mers el-Kebir to numberless creeks and inlets, or quiet lagunes accessible only to craft of shallow draught and to pilots familiar with the dangerous shoals. The vagaries of weather could also bring destruction on a stranger, for strong offshore winds might keep him from closing in on a corsair base but allow a sudden sortie from it, whilst the fierce northerlies blowing up out of a clear sky more than once dashed an invasion force against the rocky coast. Besides such natural defences, the steep mountain sides provided excellent look-outs from which unsuspecting prey could be spotted far out to sea. Jutting headlands performed a similar function. Cape Bon was a particularly good vantage point from which to watch for ships bound for the southern ports of Sicily. Here Europe and Africa come within a hundred miles of each other, and all traffic between the western and eastern basins of the Mediterranean must risk this dangerous passage, unless they chose the northern detour through the Straits of Messina. Nor did the corsairs operate only from their own coast. Strategically placed islands, deserted or thinly populated, could be held temporarily whilst the corsairs lay in wait. Formentera thus became a favourite base for raids around the Balearics, the Lipari islands against Calabria and northern Sicily, and San Pietro against Sardinia. This greatly increased the range of the corsairs' operations and allowed them to intercept ships not only off the Barbary coast, but when plying between one South European country and another, or even between two ports in the same country.

Much of Europe's trade moved through the western Mediterranean, for transport by land was slow, costly and difficult. Following the fall of Constantinople in 1453, and then with the wealth flowing from the discovery of America, the western basin of the Mediterranean grew in importance over the eastern. And as the shipping lines criss-crossed the inland sea more thickly, so the corsairs found an ever fatter livelihood. Trade and piracy increased together, the latter battening upon the former, not strangling it entirely, for that would have spelt the ruin of the corsairs as well as those who lived by legitimate commerce, but creaming off prize cargoes which then often found their way back into the mercantile system through sale to those countries with whom the corsairs were not at the time openly at war.

This system did not develop overnight, nor were its origins confined to the Barbary states which brought it to perfection. Piracy, the parasite of commerce, had its roots deep in the traditional way of Mediterranean life. The Christians practised it in the Middle Ages and continued to apply some forms of it down to the eighteenth century. Malta, built up as a bastion against Turkish and Barbary aggression, was itself a base for Christian corsairs. Livorno, familiar to the mariners and merchants of northern Europe under its anglicized name of Leghorn, had a slave market scarcely less important than that of Algiers. Aragon, in particular, knew how to combine, or alternate, trade with piracy long before Christendom had begun to tremble at the name of Barbary. Since the middle of the thirteenth century, the Aragonese pursued a policy of peaceful penetration of central and eastern Maghrib. Catalan mercenaries served the Zayanid princes, heirs to much of the Almohad empire, and their commander acted as a sort of consul who furthered Aragonese commercial interests and was recognized as chief of all the Christian communities permitted to live in the Zayanid domains. Aragonese *funduks*, or European compounds, existed in Oran, the chief port for Zayanid trade with Europe, in Bougie, and in Tunis, where the Hafsids assumed the Almohad mantle in the thirteenth century. Under that tolerant dynasty the Christians were allowed to practise their religion freely, and Dominican and Franciscan friars were even able to carry on some missionary work.

Perhaps it was the expectation that this part at least of North Africa was ripe for reconversion to Christianity that led to an abandonment of the policy of coexistence and peaceful penetration in favour of violent methods. In 1270 King Louis IX of France landed with his crusading army and laid siege to Tunis. He died soon afterwards and peace was concluded. Jaime the Conqueror, king of Aragon, had refused to take part in this Eighth Crusade, as he saw that it could only harm his country's commercial interests. These continued to flourish until the early part of the following century, when an increase in Hafsid power provoked a recrudescence of Moslem aggression which in turn led to a switch of policy by Aragon, and its official sponsorship of corsair activity. The famous Moslem historian Ibn Khaldun, who studied in Tunis, refers to Bougie as a well-known centre of Moslem piracy in 1364. Mahdiya, another Hafsid stronghold, became so troublesome in this respect that a joint force from Sicily, Genoa, France and Aragon attempted unsuccessfully to capture it in 1390.

For much of the fifteenth century Spain was too distracted by internal strife to push on with the Reconquest at home or pursue a forward policy in Africa. But Portugal seized the opportunity to gain ground south of the Straits. In 1415 Ceuta was seized in an unprovoked attack, its Moorish inhabitants being slaughtered or enslaved. King Duarte then consulted the Pope as to whether an assault on Tangier would be justified; the Pope advised against it, but it was attacked none the less, though without success. Well before the end of the century, the Portuguese had established footholds along the Atlantic coast of Morocco—at Casablanca, Arzila and Tangier—as they secured their route down the west coast of Africa to the Cape of Good Hope. In Spain, too, in the last quarter of the fifteenth century, the Reconquest revived under the Catholic Monarchs. The fall of Granada, the buffer state between Christian Spain and Moslem Africa, stimulated the fanatical religiosity of both Christians and Moors. It was in this mood of heightened militancy and resentment that the Morisco refugees began to disembark on the Barbary coast in 1492.

There had been intermittent movements of population in both directions between al-Andalus and the Maghrib ever since the first Moslem detachments crossed the straits into Spain more than seven centuries before. Sometimes the Moriscos emigrated to Africa of their own free will, sometimes they were deported by the stern Almoravid and Almohad warriors who had come to their defence but looked upon their coreligionists as little better than the Christians. The settlers had proved their worth, and were now to do so more than ever, as artisans, masons, skilled cultivators and soldiers. Tunis, Algiers, Oran, Bougie and other towns, which acquired considerable Morisco communities, began to experience a new prosperity, whilst places which had suffered greatly in the wars which followed the break-up of the Almohad empire rose again from their ruins. But soon reports began to reach them which fanned the resentment the Moriscos nursed against the Spaniards - and sharpened their thirst for revenge. The guarantees given to the Moslems who had stayed behind in Granada were being disregarded and they were being persecuted and forced to accept Christian baptism. The liberal provisions of the Capitulations were abandoned in favour of harsh measures to expedite the Moriscos' assimilation into the religion and way of life of their conquerors. The outcome was a general rising of the Moriscos in the Alpujarras mountains round Granada and a fresh wave of repression and deportation.

After 1500 reprisal raids against the coasts of southern and south-eastern Spain began to grow frequent. These were carried out chiefly by galliots, swift and light craft rowed by the raiders, many of them Moriscos, and built either by the latter or by Christian slaves under Moslem supervision. By the spring of 1505, a dozen such rovers were operating from Mers el-Kebir alone. They sacked the outskirts of Elche and Alicante and carried out a daring night attack on the shipping in Málaga harbour. The frequency and insolence of these raids and the indignant alarm caused by the number of men, women and children carried off into slavery renewed popular clamour in Spain for the Reconquest to be carried forward into Africa. Alexander VI had given the papal blessing to such a crusade in 1494, but King Ferdinand's interests in Italy, together with the exciting prospects opened up by the discovery of the New World, diverted attention for a time from Africa, though Cardinal Ximénez, the queen's influential confessor and later Archbishop of Toledo, never ceased to call for a renewal of the crusade. Queen Isabella died in 1504, but her testament charged Spain with the vigorous prosecution of its sacred mission. Ships and land forces were assembled and the task finally taken in hand.

The weak and divided Barbary states found themselves very much at the mercy of a Spain irritated rather than seriously harmed by the corsair raids stimulated by the disaffected Moriscos. Mers el-Kebir fell; and then, in 1509, Oran, which was to remain in Spanish hands for two centuries. The following year Bougie and Tripoli were taken. Other towns found them-

selves compelled to pay tribute, Algiers being in addition
required to surrender a rocky islet, the Peñón, on which the
Spaniards built a fort to command its harbour. Spain seemed
to have drawn the teeth of the Barbary corsairs. But her
position was in reality far less secure than it appeared. Her
African strong-points, or *presidios*, were not used as spring-
boards for the effective conquest and pacification of the whole
area, still less as bases for European colonization. They remained garrison towns, dependent on a dilatory government
for their supplies, reinforcements and for much of their food.
They were frequently besieged, and sometimes captured, by
the hostile tribes whom they were supposed to overawe, and
their sea communications could be easily cut. Their garrisons
dwindled as the result of unsuccessful raids into the interior and
frequent desertions. The dream of an African crusade faded
with the retirement of the ageing Ximénez, to leave the
precariousness of the Spanish hold on Barbary startlingly
demonstrated by an unforeseen and formidable new factor—the
advent of Turkish military and naval power in the western
Mediterranean.

Chance rather than design—or, pious Moslems might have
said, the hand of Allah himself—seemed to have brought about
this accession of strength to the Ottoman empire as the latter
prepared to challenge Europe's leading Catholic power for the
mastery of the Mediterranean. The two remarkable men who
were its instruments had come from the Greek island of
Mytilene, and were the sons—it seems—of a Turkish father
and a Christian mother. They took to the sea as corsairs, 'Aruj,
the elder, being captured and chained for a time to the oar of a
Christian galley before recovering his freedom and deciding to
seek his fortune further west. Establishing themselves around
1504 in Tunis, with the blessing of its Hafsid ruler, the
adventurers soon began to reap rich rewards. The first prizes
seized by their two light galliots were a couple of large papal
galleys; soon afterwards there followed a Spanish galleon
carrying 500 soldiers and treasure for the payment of troops in
Italy. The captives were enslaved and the ships dismantled so
that more galliots could be built from their timbers. By 1510, as
the Spaniards strengthened their hold on the Barbary coast
from the west, establishing *presidios* and forcing the Moslem

princes into vassalage, the brothers shifted the base of their operations further east to the island of Djerba. Their fleet had now grown to twelve galliots.

The Moslem rulers who had been ousted by the Spaniards or who looked for some means of escaping from vassalage, began to turn to the brilliantly successful rovers. Twice, at the invitation of its exiled ruler, Bougie was attacked, but the Spaniards managed to beat off the raiders. 'Aruj withdrew to Djerba where he set his Christian slaves to the task of rebuilding his battered fleet. An expedition commanded by the Italian Admiral Andrea Doria attempted to reassert Christian authority by carrying out a punitive action against Tunis and destroyed the shipping in its harbour of La Goletta. From Djerba, 'Aruj moved to a new base at Djidjelli and continued to harass the Spaniards, now at the height of their power in Barbary. With the death of King Ferdinand in 1516 the scene began to change. The Algerians, who had been chafing under the menance of the Spanish fort on the Peñón, decided that the moment had come to cast off their yoke. They refused to continue paying tribute, and their ruler, Shaikh Salim, appealed to 'Aruj for help. After securing Sharshal, to the west of Algiers, executing its ruler (one of his old corsair captains) whose men were then incorporated into his own troops, he marched on Algiers, where he meted out a similar fate to the Shaikh. He was to be the first of a new line of redoubtable corsair rulers.

Cardinal Ximénez, now regent of Spain and still fired with the vision of his country's mission in Africa, sent an expedition of 10,000 men to reduce the rebellious vassals to obedience. It was repulsed on landing, with the loss of some 400 prisoners, whilst a storm completed the havoc. 'Aruj lost no time in striking against the princes who had lent themselves, however unwillingly, to the Spanish alliance. Tenes was occupied, and then the important inland city of Tlemcen. But meanwhile the Spaniards in Oran had received reinforcements and sallied out to cut the enemy's extended lines of communication. 'Aruj withdrew hastily from Tlemcen but was overtaken and slain.

His brother, who had been left in charge at Algiers, now assumed power. The Europeans knew him as Barbarossa, a nickname they had first given to 'Aruj on account of his ruddy beard; the Moslems were to confer on him the more honourable title of Khair al-Din, Defender of Religion, in recognition of the untold damage he came to inflict on the enemies of Islam (Plate 4). As general and admiral the second Barbarossa proved at least the equal of his brother; as statesman and administrator he was far superior. Despite the precariousness of his position in Algiers, he seems to have seized this opportunity to send envoys to the Ottoman sultan to report developments and make formal offer of suzerainty over the conquests he and his brother had made. The sultan, who had just completed the subjection of Egypt and welcomed this further extension of influence, replied by appointing him Beylerbey, or Governor-General, and sending him a contingent of 2,000 janissaries and a train of artillery. It was also announced that any volunteers who wished to enlist in Barbary should enjoy a janissary's privileges. This stimulated a steady flow of recruits from Turkey and the Levant and provided a military backbone for the Barbary states which was to link them firmly for many years to the Porte.

Spain was slow in following up the advantage offered by the death of 'Aruj. By the time a new expedition was ready to sail against Algiers (1519) Barbarossa had strengthened his defences sufficiently to secure its defeat and was soon taking the initiative again. Tenes and Sharshal were brought to heel, Bône, Constantine and other towns conquered. His captains harried the Spanish coast in league with the disaffected Morisco population. They raided the Balearics, where seven galleys returning from the coronation of the Emperor Charles V in Italy were intercepted, the commanding general being amongst those killed and his son amongst the many prisoners taken. Finally, the Peñón, which had long been a thorn in the flesh of the Algerians, was captured. Its masonry was dismantled and used by the army of enslaved Christians for the construction of a long mole linking the islet on which the fort had stood with the mainland, and so providing an ampler anchorage for the corsair ships. An expedition commanded by Andrea Doria was defeated at Sharshal, due largely to the indiscipline of the Christian troops and the blowing up of a sudden storm. In 1533, Barbarossa was called to Constantinople to reorganize the sultan's fleet, which had hitherto proved no match for Doria in the eastern Mediterranean. Before long it had won the notable naval victory at Prevesa (1538) and extended its operations into the central Mediterranean, where the coasts of the Tyrrhenian Sea bore the brunt of its depredations. Barbarossa himself turned back to Africa to seize Tunis from the Hafsids who had given him and his brother protection at the outset of their brilliant corsair career.

The greater part of the Barbary coast had now been brought under Turkish rule. The capture of Tunis constituted a particular threat to Spain's position in Sicily and southern Italy and meant that the Moslems now dominated the narrow passage between the eastern and western parts of the Mediterranean. Charles V resolved to counter the threat by moving first against Tunis and then against Algiers. The assault on Tunis (1535) proved successful, largely thanks to a simultaneous rising of 12,000 Christian captives who broke their chains and joined up with the emperor's troops advancing from La Goletta. Barbarossa made his escape to Bône, where he had taken the precaution of leaving some of his ships. From there, instead of fleeing to Constantinople, the indomitable corsair made a damaging counter-incursion into Christian territory, ravaging the Balearics and sacking Port Mahon, whose 6,000 inhabitants he carried off in triumph to Algiers. Only then did he sail back to Constantinople to spend the next years scouring the Adriatic and the Aegean, and ending his days in high honour at the Ottoman court.

In 1541, six years after the capture of Tunis, Charles V launched his blow against Algiers, where Barbarossa's resolute deputy Hassan had been left in command. The Christian armada, which the emperor commanded in person, was one of the most formidable ever assembled. It consisted of more than 500 ships and 24,000 of the imperial troops—Spaniards, Italians, Germans, and the Knights of St John, who had installed themselves in Malta after being driven out of Rhodes by the Turks. The expedition reached Algiers and had scarcely disembarked the army and only a small portion of the supplies before a torrential and prolonged downpour turned the approaches to the city into a sea of mud, whilst a furious north-westerly gale threatened to dash Doria's ships against the coast. Demoralized by cold, hunger and the rain which prevented the effective use of their firearms, the troops were forced to re-embark, harassed by sorties from the city and attacks by local tribesmen. A rich booty of arms and prisoners was left behind. Amongst the many who suffered shipwreck we read of an English volunteer, Thomas Chaloner, who, when his hands were numb with cold, escaped drowning by 'laying hold with his teeth on a cable, which was cast out of the next galley, not without breaking and losse of certaine of his teeth, [and] at length recovered himselfe, and returned home into his country in safety'.[1]

The next thirty years saw a grim confrontation between the two great empires, the Spanish and the Turkish, in which, more often than not, the Crescent seemed to be gaining the upper hand. Only after the failure of their siege of Malta (1565) and their defeat by the combined fleets of the Holy Alliance at Lepanto (1571) did it begin to look as if the Turks had passed their apogee. The Barbary corsairs, during this time, operated both on their own account and as units of the Turkish armadas. They took part in the operations against Malta where Dragut, the famous corsair chief from Tripoli, lost his life. They formed part of the Turkish order of battle at Lepanto, in which the Algerian corsair Ochiali acquitted himself brilliantly, wresting a partial victory from the general defeat and afterwards restoring the sultan's shattered fleet to much of its former strength. Algiers remained relatively little affected by these general reverses. Only a few years later, its slave-prisons were full of the victors of Lepanto, Spain's greatest writer amongst them. An alliance with the king of France, the Spaniards' bitterest rival, gave the corsairs the use of French ports for their activities in the northern Mediterranean. Their ships, which operated in large squadrons, particularly during the decade following Lepanto, could thus the more easily carry out their terrible depredations against the shores and shipping of Italy and Spain.

The Barbary states (excluding Morocco, which remained free of Turkish control) were now organized as three 'Regencies' —Tunis, Tripoli and Algiers, the latter pre-eminent amongst them—the Porte preferring them to retain their separate identities rather than combine in any larger grouping which might aspire to independence. The term for 'Regency' was *ojaq*, a word also used to denote the corps of janissaries—a sufficient indication of the dominant part which that form of military power came to play in sustaining the authority of the ruler and, with time, in dominating and even appointing him. The janissaries' influence was balanced by that of the *raïs* or corsair captains who had their own corporation (*taïfa*), the head of which was the High Admiral of the State. The *raïs* originally excluded the janissaries from participating in the cruises which brought Algiers and its sister cities their chief prosperity; later, the janissaries were given responsibility for boarding and capturing the prizes, and this partnership undoubtedly increased the dread efficacy of corsair operations. A third component, of exceptional importance in the rise of the Barbary states, was represented by the renegades who furnished an endless stream of recruits to both janissaries and *raïs*, and produced some of their ablest chiefs. Other heterogeneous elements were assigned a subordinate place; the Morisco immigrants and their descendants; the *spahis*, called up as cavalry in times of need; the *kouloughlis*, sons of native women and janissaries, whose growing numbers and local loyalties came to represent a threat to the *corps d'élite*; and the restless Kabyle tribes of the interior. The latter would rally to repel a Christian invasion but were otherwise in a state of more or less open rebellion against the janissaries who were sent out to collect tribute from them. Lastly, there were the Christian slaves, whose sinews supplied power for the propulsion of the galleys and for the maintenance and extension of the defences, and who were always ready—as they had shown at Tunis—to turn on their masters whenever they could seize the chance.

But if the Regencies had their potential fifth column, Spain's was on a far more extensive and dangerous scale. Despite the harsh repression of the Moriscos' rebellion round Granada in 1500, and the deportation of many of them to Castile, they were still to be found in large communities in southern Spain, and still more so along the eastern coast, to Valencia and beyond. They constituted alien enclaves whose loyalty was to the Islamic world on the far side of the Mediterranean. Since 1502 they had been given the choice of conversion or exile. Most stayed on, nominally Christian but in reality as tenaciously

Moslem as before. A clandestine two-way traffic with Barbary was in full swing. Morisco *émigrés* would return as pilots or land-guides for large-scale raiding expeditions, or to carry out espionage or smaller incursions of their own. Some came with light galliots which they would hide in a familiar creek or leave buried in the sand. The raiders would then melt away into the countryside, sheltering with friends and relatives, indistinguishable in dress and speech from the Christian population, until seizing the moment to carry off their prey—a fisherman tending his nets, a party of women working in the vineyards, a priest or merchant travelling along the highway—and return with them to Barbary. The intelligence they were able to gather about shipping movements was often of the greatest value to the lurking corsair squadrons. Sometimes, too, they would arrange the voluntary evacuation of Morisco families to North Africa. In 1529, before sailing on to Formentera and the capture of the seven Spanish galleys returning from Italy, the corsairs landed by arrangement on the Valencian coast to take off 200 disaffected Moriscos from the estates of the Conde de Oliva.

In the 1560s the Spanish authorities tried to solve the Morisco question by increasing the pressures for cultural and religious assimilation. At the same time evidence began to come to light that the Moriscos were actively soliciting help from the Barbary states and the Porte. Agents were taken and correspondence intercepted. The Turks were invited to land in Spain once they had succeeded in capturing Malta. The Moriscos' grievances were laid before the Mufti of Constantinople and the Grand Signior himself. Agents went to and fro between the Morisco conspirators and Ochiali, the ruler of Algiers. But neither the Porte nor the Barbary states proved willing to underwrite the forthcoming rebellion whole-heartedly. Ochiali was more interested in strengthening his own position in North Africa, and he confined himself to announcing that any volunteers who wished to do so might go to fight in Spain. When the rebellion finally broke out in 1568 the help received from Barbary was not on the scale the conspirators had hoped for. Some Moriscos, and even a few janissaries, did cross over to fight, and some shiploads of arms, food and supplies were sent, but the rebels, like any guerrilla bands, depended largely on what they could seize from the enemy. In the bitter fighting, which lasted until the autumn of 1570, many Spanish prisoners were taken and sent to Barbary as slaves, often in exchange for arms, on the basis of 'a Christian for a musket'. The hill-top town of Saldas near Almería became for a while the centre for this flourishing barter.[2] As the brutal repression put in hand by Don Juan of Austria, King Philip's young half-brother, began to take effect, the appeals which reached Barbary grew more desperate. 'If you fail to send us help, you will have to answer for it on the Day of Judgment', fulminated Aben-Abóo, the hard-pressed leader of the rebellion.[3] But Ochiali, intent on extending his power to Tunis and alarmed by reports that the Christians were planning the formation of a Holy League, made no move. He saw that Barbary must husband its resources to meet the threat which was soon to face the Ottoman empire at Lepanto.

After that great Christian victory, with the Morisco revolt in Spain firmly crushed, the Barbary states had reason to fear some new descent from the Iberian peninsula. When the blow fell, it was not from Spain but from Portugal, under her rash young crusading King Sebastian. His impossible dream of winning Morocco for the Cross was shattered in 1578 at the disaster of Alcázarquivir, where the king perished with the *élite* of his army. The slave-markets of Barbary were flooded with Portuguese prisoners, whilst two years later Portugal herself, with her African possessions, passed into the hands of Philip II of Spain.

Throughout the length of the Maghrib, from the Atlantic to the borders of Egypt, Spain and the Barbary states confronted each other. The Ottoman empire, still the only power capable of matching imperial Spain, had other preoccupations. She was heavily engaged with Persia in the east, and her eyes were fixed on Vienna, the prize of eastern and central Europe. Her direct influence over the Barbary states was to grow successively weaker. Spain, too, particularly after the annexation of Portugal, turned increasingly outward to the Atlantic world.[4] But if the two giants thus found themselves relatively disengaged, this did not mean that calm had come to the Mediterranean. The corsairs could only live by war—not the war of pitched battles, but of incessant guerrilla warfare, sudden descents on undefended coasts, surprise attacks on towns and villages, the seizure of fishing boats and coasting vessels, the cutting out of laggards from straggling convoys. For such tactics, the seventeenth century was to prove a new age of opportunity.

4

Corsairs and Captives

How did the Barbary corsairs manage to operate so long and so successfully against powers which came vastly to outstrip them in size and strength? Apart from furnishing them with secure bases within striking distance of the main Mediterranean lines of communication, nature had endowed them with few advantages for such a role. They had little wood, except for some forests round Bougie and Sharshal, and they relied largely on the prizes they captured, which they would either incorporate in their fleets as they were, adapt to their own requirements, or simply break up in order to re-use their timbers. They depended for anchors, cordage, canvas and similar essentials on what they could obtain by trade or tribute, and for shipwrights, carpenters, sailmakers, caulkers and other craftsmen on their Christian slaves and renegades. But the qualities they required from their own ships, and the tactics they perfected, were of their own devising; superior speed and manoeuvrability.

The traditional warship of the Mediterranean was the galley, the basic design of which had not changed greatly since Roman times. In length it measured some 180 feet, and in breadth about 16, its greater part being taken up by 18 to 24 banks of benches to which the oarsmen were chained. Down the centre ran a raised gangway along which the boatswain or overseer (*cómitre*) and his assistant would stride, pitilessly plying their whips to drive the slaves to ever greater exertions. The horrors of this living hell—whether on board a Moslem or a Christian galley—have become legendary. The naked slaves, four or five to a fifteen-foot oar, not seated but leaping to throw their whole weight behind the stroke, would sometimes toil for between ten to twenty hours at a stretch to overhaul a quarry or escape a pursuer, sleeping together in the same cramped space, and nourished only on dry rusks, an occasional plate of gruel, and sips of vinegar and water. We read of fainting slaves being lashed back to consciousness, having their noses or ears cropped for indiscipline, and of exhausted bodies heaved unceremoniously overboard. These horrors could, and did, occur in the fury of the chase and at the hands of a sadistic overseer. But in general the aim was to keep the oarsmen in condition to get the most out of them at a crucial moment. When there was no question of combat, the lateen sail would be hoisted and the slaves would be left to nurse their scars and sores, for scurvy, caused by their meagre, deficient diet, probably wrought more havoc amongst them than the overseer's whip.

The corsairs' galleys were lighter and faster than the Christians'. They were one-masted instead of two, lightly gunned and provisioned, with a superstructure stripped down to the minimum (Plate 2). They were scrupulously maintained and so carefully careened and greased that they could glide through the water, the Spanish chroniclers tell us, like fish, stealing so suddenly upon their prey and approaching from the quarters where the enemy's guns could not be brought to bear, that the slower, clumsier Christian vessel found herself hopelessly out-manoeuvred. The corsairs' tactics were to grapple with their prize and overpower it. At their galley's bow was a powerful metal ram, and behind it the poop on which was mounted a small gun discharged to clear the enemy's decks before boarding. The fighting men, armed with muskets, bows and scimitars, mustered there ready to leap aboard and capture their prey. Should the Christians, on closer inspection, seem more than a match, the corsairs could break off the attack and rely on their superior speed to make off with little fear of capture. They also made use of smaller, lighter craft called galliots, with 17–23 banks of oarsmen, and still smaller boats such as *fregatas*, *fustas* and *fellucas*. These were rowed not by Christian slaves, but by the corsairs themselves, and were used mainly by the Moriscos in their quick raids on the Spanish coast. Later, when the corsairs took to sail, their favourite craft was the *xebec*, a light and swift three-master, also equipped with auxiliary oars.

The corsair ship was commanded by a *raïs* or captain, who was often its owner as well, and generally a European renegade or a Turk, but seldom a Moor. The soldiers were under the orders of the Agha of Janissaries, who was consulted on the course to be set, whether or not to attack, and similar weighty questions. In addition to the other officers, each ship carried a secretary or scribe whose duty it was to keep an inventory of the goods and prisoners captured, which were later shared out according to a meticulously calculated scale. On the taking of a prize, a brief free-for-all set in, in the course of which each member of the boarding party seized for himself what he could of the clothes and personal possessions of the captives. The cargo and fixtures were left untouched for the collective share-out, whilst the ship itself was reserved originally for the Pasha, though this too was later added to the general stock of booty. Father Dan, who was in Algiers in 1634, states that the distribution was made along the following lines; 12% (10% in Tripoli, Tunis and Sallee) was first deducted in favour of the Pasha, together with 1% for upkeep of the port and $1\frac{1}{2}$% for the support of the marabouts. What remained was next divided into two parts, one for the owner or owners of the ship, the other for the ship's company. Allocations between the latter were made on the following scale; the *raïs* (in addition to anything he might get as its owner) 10, 12, or 15 parts; the Agha, master-gunner, pilot, surgeon, and other senior officers, 3 parts each; janissaries, sailors and gunners, 2 parts; Moorish auxiliaries, 1 part.[1] The slaves, of whom there might be as many as 200, would also get 1 part each, though this had to be surrendered to their owners, who might however allow them to retain a pittance. Some owners made a profitable business of hiring out their slaves for this service, as the *raïs* often had too few of his own to man the ship. Merchants, small traders, even women who sold their jewels in order to invest, sometimes joined forces to form combines or companies. A captive might therefore find himself in bondage to several masters and obliged to serve each in rotation. If the cruises brought in little, the speculators might be ruined. A prudent law, strictly enforced, required that any corsair ship sunk or captured should at once be replaced at its owners' expense and the state's naval strength thus maintained. But in general, the *corso* proved profitable, often to a sensational degree, so that Algiers and its sister-cities grew rich on the spoils of Christendom.

Algiers possessed the largest fleet. It numbered about 60 oar-propelled warships in 1530, and nearly as many in 1580. Half a century later its size had increased, and it included 'round-ships' with 25, 35 and 40 guns. Dan watched a squadron of 28—'the finest and best armed that are to be seen'—set sail to prey upon Breton, Norman and English shipping; the rest of the corsair fleet, except for a smaller squadron which left a week later for the Levant, was already at sea. He adds that Tunis had 14 warships on cruise, Tripoli only 7 or 8 out of a previous stength of 25, and Sallee 30. He estimates the total number of round-ships operating from those ports at 122, not to mention the galleys and smaller oar-propelled vessels.[2] By 1724, the number of Algerian sailing ships had dwindled to 24, but each was armed with between 32 and 52 guns; half of these had been built in Algiers itself, the rest seized from Britain, Holland and other countries. By about 1745 no more than 7 or 8 round-ships were operating from Algiers, whilst about twenty years later the French consul in Tripoli reported that the corsairs of that city had been reduced to 3 *xebecs* and 5 galliots, 3 of which had recently been lost. But the corsairs had not yet had their day; with the outbreak of the Napoleonic wars they were to enjoy an Indian summer and regain much of their old pride and prosperity.

When a *raïs* decided to try his fortune, he would first seek permission for a cruise from the ruler, the Pasha or Dey. This was never refused unless the state required his services for its defence or for a contingent to join the sultan's fleet. Once the business had become more sophisticated and treaty obligations needed to be taken into account, the ruler would issue written instructions specifying any areas to be avoided or foreign flags to be respected. The *raïs* might also apply to the consuls of those European powers with which the Regency happened to be at peace and obtain a 'passport' to safeguard him against capture or molestation by ships of those powers. He would then raise a green banner in the port and invite volunteers to enlist. Janissaries, each man bringing his arms, a blanket, and perhaps a few extra rations, would be taken on with no other remuneration than a share of the booty expected. Extra galley-slaves would be hired if needed; twelve escudos a head per cruise was the relatively high rate commonly charged by their owners. If he had the reputation of a successful corsair and prospects

seemed good, there would be no lack of volunteers, but sometimes the *raïs* had difficulty in completing the ship's company,
either because of the lack of available slaves or sailors or
because of his poor showing on previous raids; Moorish or
Negro riff-raff would then have to be engaged, some of whom
had no other means of livelihood. Preparations completed, the
corsair would fire a one-gun salute and set sail, preferably on a
Friday or a Sunday, which were accounted the most auspicious
days. On leaving Algiers harbour, slaves and corsairs alike
would salute the tomb of Sidi Beteka, the marabout whose
prayers had reputedly conjured up the storm which had
brought destruction on Charles V's army, and cry: 'Allah
give us good speed!', to which the crowd on shore would make
answer: 'May Allah send you a prize!'

Contemporary Catholic chroniclers refer derisively to the
raïs consulting 'certain divination books' as to which course they
should take, where to land, and whether or not to attack the
ships sighted. Whatever these mysterious papers may have
been—and the only man on board able to read was often the
scribe or *hodja*—superstition, as well as navigational skill and
experience, no doubt helped to determine the corsairs' tactics.
Though always ready to spring a surprise on their victims, they
tended to operate within certain broad guide-lines. The
cruising season lasted from spring to autumn, although a sortie
ventured in the winter was not unknown and would be the
more likely to catch the enemy off his guard. The cruise would
frequently be interrupted in order to put in to some island or
lonely shore where water could be taken on board and the
vessel re-greased to keep it at maximum efficiency. This was the
moment when the slaves, though heavily fettered and guarded,
might occasionally escape or be rescued through the unexpected
arrival of a stronger Christian force. The *corso* was a lottery, for
captives as well as for corsairs. None knew, on setting out,
whether he would return with fresh spoils and prisoners, or not
return at all. For the galley-slaves, there was the dread of the
certain inferno before them; but there was the excitement of the
unknown too.

For the captives-to-be an encounter with the corsairs could
only be a moment of unmitigated anguish and terror. It was for
their captain, often tricked by a false flag or by a voice hailing

him in a familiar tongue, to make the fateful decision whether to attempt resistance or surrender. If his ship was a sailing vessel and the wind favourable, he might still try to shake his pursuers off; but if oar-propelled, there was no escape, at least for his passengers, though it was by no means uncommon, if the encounter occurred near a friendly shore, for the captain to make off in a skiff in the hope that the corsairs would content themselves with his cargo and passengers. The first concern of the aggressors was not merely to rifle their captives but to take advantage of the latter's fear and demoralization to ascertain their identity and thus gauge the ransoms to be expected from them. Threats and cudgelling were fiercely applied to this end. Women were generally respected; if young, they would command the highest prices in the market or be released only for commensurate ransoms. Captured seamen were often merely placed under guard and assigned as prize crews to the craft they had been handling or for other duties.

Captives who managed to keep their heads concentrated on trying to conceal a few coins or valuables about them and, if they were persons of rank and fortune, to convince their captors of their humble station. Personal papers would be destroyed and fine clothing stripped off. We hear of one titled Englishman changing clothes with his valet and keeping up the deception until first he, and then his pretended master, had secured their ransoms (see p. 139). To swallow a gold coin or two was a common enough expedient, which the corsairs would attempt to counter by holding the suspect upside down and giving him a good shake. One case is on record of a French numismatist who, having suffered one spell of slavery in Algiers and finding himself again in danger of capture, swallowed twenty of his most precious coins; the attackers sheered off, and though the gold lay heavy upon his stomach until he was able to relieve himself of it back in France, he stoutly declared that 'anyone who has once known the rigours of captivity would have swallowed not only the coins, but the ship itself, if that were possible'.[3]

The corsairs made their largest hauls of captives not at sea but on land. Incursions against the mainland of Spain grew less frequent after the expulsion of the Moriscos in the early seventeenth century, but the Italian islands and seaboard remained disastrously vulnerable for another two centuries. Barbarossa Khair al-Din and Dragut were responsible for the most fearsome of these earlier incursions. But even before Barbarossa's day, Pope Leo X, whilst out hunting, had only just escaped being seized by the corsair Kurdogli by galloping post-haste back to Rome. Two years later his admiral Paolo Vettori was among the many captives carried off to Tunis. Barbarossa brought to that city 5,000 captives from Minorca alone. In 1534, after devastating the country round Naples, he led an attack on Fondi with the object of capturing its ruler, the Countess Giulia Gonzaga, celebrated for her beauty, piety and learning, and presenting her as a spectacular addition to the Grand Signior's harem. Fondi was laid in ruins and many of its inhabitants killed or enslaved, but the young countess was roused from sleep just in time to escape in her night-shift. A dozen years later, the Gulf of Naples was ravaged by the no less terrible Dragut. So great was the number of men and woman taken that it was impossible to transport them all back to Barbary. A white flag was raised, and the corsairs invited their families and friends to buy back the captives on the spot. We hear of a similar deal being arranged outside Cadiz in 1559.[4]

The destruction of a village and the enslavement of its population might be the work of a traitor bent on revenge. This was particularly the case in Calabria, where the vendetta was traditional and the proximity of the Tunisian corsairs a constant temptation to reprisals. A boatman of Nicotera called Giovanni Andrea Capria, whose daughter had been seduced by the feudal lord, offered himself as guide to seven boat-loads of corsairs who descended upon that place in 1638. In the course of the foray, Capria is said to have killed the dishonoured girl with his own hands, but to have himself been seized and hanged from the bow of a captured galley. Six years later we hear of another renegade pursuing his vendetta by instigating a raid against his home province of Catanzaro, and following it up the next year by a veritable invasion with thirty ships and 6,000 men. Another spectacular revenge by a renegade was that achieved in 1798 by a citizen of Carloforte, the chief town on the island of San Pietro off Sardinia, who was responsible for enabling the Tunisians to carry off about 900 of its inhabitants, most of them women and children.[5]

The raid over, the corsairs returned home in triumph with their captives and booty. A salute of guns announced their approach; the more successful the cruise, the more thunderous the gunfire. The whole city would come alive with excitement. Almost every section of the population had some stake in the enterprise: the Dey and his high officials, who awaited their share; the ship-owners, entrepreneurs and small shareholders who had financed it; the merchants eager to buy and resell the plunder, and the speculators who hoped to make a similar profit out of the human merchandise; the tavern- and brothel-keepers preparing to cater for the free-spending sailors and janissaries. As the corsairs approached the harbour, the *limam raïs* or port captain would come out in his barge to get particulars of the prizes and hurry back to the palace to report. Once alongside, the galley-slaves, before being unshackled, secured the oars with ropes and heaved them overboard; these would then be collected, together with the rudders and sails of all sailing-vessels in port, and taken to well-guarded storerooms to forestall any attempt by the slaves to make off with a ship. Whilst a start was made on drawing up an inventory of the captured goods, the captives were led ashore. This was the moment when the slave-informers went into action, ingratiating themselves and feigning friendship with the new arrivals in the hope of worming out of them the maximum amount of ransom-money they hoped to be able to raise, which information was then made available, at a price, to interested dealers. Other slaves crowded round, anxious to see whether there were any friends or relatives amongst them, and to learn news of their homeland (Plate 1).

The first sight of Algiers, where the majority of the new-comers were to live out their captivity, may well have inspired wonder as well as dread. Rows of white-washed houses, flat-roofed and set close together like the tiers of a gigantic amphitheatre, rose up the steep hillside to the Casbah fortress which dominated the city. The ramparts which enclosed it were defended by numerous small bastions and broken by several gateways. On the landward side was the Bab Azoun, through which all traffic and travellers bound for the interior passed. On the west, the Bab el-Oued opened out onto a level expanse of ground normally used for the wares of wood- and charcoal-merchants, but sometimes cleared for the grisly purpose of public burnings; the hillside beyond was dotted with pleasant country houses standing in the midst of gardens and orchards worked by Christian slaves. The Marine Gate stood at the end of the great mole built by slave labour to link the city with the islet which the Spaniards had once fortified to keep the corsairs in check. A few hundred yards to the east was the Gate of the Fishermen leading to a strip of shore where the fishing boats were beached and warships built and repaired. Behind the ramparts, the lines of terraced roofs were broken by an occasional larger building—the Jenina, or Dey's palace, the mosques, the public baths, the janissary barracks, the bagnios or slave-prisons. From out to sea, hardly a chink could be seen in this jumble of shining masonry, for the streets were exceedingly narrow. There was only one thoroughfare of any width which traversed the city from the Bab el-Oued to the Bab Azoun and served for some of its length as the Bedestan, or slave-market. Here most of the captives would undergo their degrading initiation into Algerian slavery.

In the last years of the corsairs' rule, when the European powers had grown strong enough to enforce compliance with treaty restrictions on the enslavement of their respective nationals, the consuls would have the right to be present at the preliminary examination of new captives. Those who could prove that they were citizens of a nation with which the Barbary states were nominally at peace, even if they had been travelling as passengers on an enemy ship, would normally be released; but if they had taken service on such a ship, the Dey would claim them as lawfully enslaved. Disputes on such dubious cases were frequent and bitter. Captives who could not make good a claim to immunity would be sent to the bagnio or confined by the *raïs* in a room or courtyard of his own house. From there they might be hawked around to several likely buyers before being taken out to the Bedestan. There they were generally paraded on three successive mornings, stripped and subjected to humiliating public inspection. Professional auctioneers would take charge of them, walking them up and down, occasionally prodding them to make them show their paces by running and jumping, whilst declaiming the qualities of their merchandise and inviting bids for the auction which was held later in the day. The more valuable slaves were paraded singly, the rest in batches. Their inspection, and the assessment of their potential value, was a skilled business in which Jewish middlemen specialized. Attention was particularly directed to the state of the teeth—for if bought as galley-slaves, they would be required to subsist on rock-like ship's biscuit— and their hands. The latter could reveal whether the men were used to heavy work or were of gentle birth; palmists also purported to read the lines of their hands to tell whether the slave was likely to give his master a long lifetime of service and to bring him good fortune.

Women captives were treated more decorously, the distinguished and attractive amongst them being confined in a latticed apartment where they could be inspected with greater intimacy. Joseph Pitts, an English slave who accompanied his master on travels to other Moslem lands, observed that in the Cairo slave-market

> although the women and maidens are veiled, yet the chapmen have liberty to view their faces, and to put their fingers into their mouths to feel their teeth; and also to feel their breasts. And further, as I have been informed, they are sometimes permitted by the sellers (in a modest way) to be searched whether they are Virgins or no.[6]

Whether the same liberties were permitted to Barbary slave-dealers we are not told, but it seems unlikely that the Algerians would be more backward than the Egyptians in finding out just what they were buying. Women destined for ransom were placed under the care of a special official and closely guarded until their release was arranged. Terrible outrages nevertheless sometimes occurred. One grim case, in which violence was met by violence, is recorded by the chaplain to the British consulate. In 1747, a batch of officers belonging to the Hibernian Regiment—Irishmen in the service of Spain—were captured and brought to Algiers with their womenfolk. One of the latter, a Mrs Jones, was assaulted in the street by a janissary and took

1   Christian slaves in Algiers

2   A Barbary war galley

3   A Mediterranean round-ship

refuge in a loft. The janissary seized one of her two small children and threatened to wound it unless she came down. When the mother refused, he severed one of the child's hands with his scimitar and threw it up at her. There was a broken millstone in the loft which the beleaguered woman managed to throw down, and with it broke the Turk's leg. He retaliated by murdering the child. The distraught mother heaved the rest of the stone down on him, and whilst the janissary was lying senseless on the ground, took his scimitar and cut off his head. She then gathered up the mutilated corpse of her child and gave herself up.[7]

The deals concluded in the Bedestan were only provisional. The slaves had next to be brought before the Dey, who had the right to take any of them he fancied at the price their owners had just paid for them. This price varied enormously according to the laws of supply and demand and the nature of the goods offered. After the defeat of one large Spanish force, the haul was so great that slaves were said to have been sold off 'for the cost of an onion'. The old and sickly would go for very little, whilst robust young men capable of many years' service at the oar, artisans and craftsmen, particularly shipwrights, sail-makers, gunners or cannon-founders, lively young boys and nubile girls, priests, senior officers and nobles, from whom a high ransom might be wrung, could command high prices. Slaves frequently changed hands, each time to the profit of their masters, many of whom were in the business purely as specu-lators. But after the second sale, in the Dey's presence, the new slave could generally tell what fate had in store for him. He would find himself either the property of a private owner, assigned to the generally less onerous tasks of the household and gardens, or else to some *raïs* or to the Dey himself, where back-breaking toil at the oar or in the stone quarries was generally his lot. These state-owned or beylik slaves had little hope of being ransomed and saw themselves condemned to drag out their lives in the bagnios under the harsh conditions which we shall shortly be examining. The fate of the others depended largely on the type of master who happened to have bought them. But acquisition by a good master might in itself prove a slave's undoing, for it could arouse the dangerous envy of his comrades. Cases were not unknown of desperate and ruthless men killing or maiming a fellow slave in the knowledge that such crimes were rarely punished by the offender's execution. Instead, his owner was more often held to blame and made to pay compensation by ceding his own slave in compensation to the dead man's master.[8]

For the slave who undertook to raise a ransom, bondage could be made either light or intolerable. If it was long in coming, or insufficient to satisfy his master's greed, the slave might be heavily fettered, half starved, mercilessly beaten, and immured in the foulest dungeons. The aim was to bring maximum pressure upon him to produce the ransom demanded without causing his death, which would have destroyed his owner's investment. But if he could satisfy his master that an acceptable ransom was on its way, and pay a monthly fee from remittances or loans, he could be exempted from labour and even from confinement. The wealthiest of these *paga-lunars* set up house with their own mistresses and horses, and with ample food and drink, so that they lived almost as well whilst technically still slaves as when they were free men in their own country. At a more modest level, a craftsman might put his skills to good use in the city, sharing the profits with his master and forming a sort of business partnership with him. One class of slave which seems to have been specially well treated was composed of those assigned to the barracks where the janissaries, each with his own room and a slave to cook and wait upon him, were housed. Other fortunate slaves were dressed and looked after so well that 'they have as much, or more, authority in their households as their own masters. They sleep in the same room, eat together, and are cared for and cherished like children'.[9] Such favourites, because of their abilities or personal attractions, were clearly on the way, if prepared to do so, to leave their servile status altogether and to gain admission into the special category of renegades at which we shall be looking more closely.

A sexual element often entered into the relationship between master and slave. Sodomy was certainly widespread, and the Redemptionist Fathers are always complaining that young captives would be quickly corrupted and become addicted to the practice, thus making them ready converts to Islam. Father Haedo, the Benedictine monk who is one of our best sources for conditions in Algiers in the late sixteenth century, declares that

> the man who keeps more male concubines (*garzónes*) is held in greater honour, and guards them more closely than his own wives and daughters, except on Fridays and feast days when they send them out to parade through the streets richly attired. Then all the gallants of the city come together, and many who are reputed to be grave men, to court them, offering them bouquets of flowers and disclosing the ardours of their passion. A man who has a son must guard him, if he wishes to keep him from this vice, and watch over him with as many eyes as Argos, for the boy will quickly find lovers who make much of him, send him presents, and accost him in the streets. No *alcaide* goes abroad, no Turk sets out on campaign, no corsair on a cruise, without his *garzón*, who cooks for him, keeps him company and shares his bed. To sin with them in broad daylight and in the sight of everyone causes no surprise. Many Turks and renegades, when full grown and old, not only have no wish to marry but boast that they have never known a woman in all their lives.[10]

The chief meeting places for homosexuals were the barbers' shops, where patrons would gather to pay court to perfumed young attendants 'as if they were the most beautiful and distinguished ladies in the world'. Pitts, writing a century and a quarter later, paints a similar picture. It was as common in Algiers, he observed, for men to fall in love with boys, as for men in England to fall in love with women. 'I have seen many,' he adds, 'when they have been drunk, that have given themselves deep gashes on their arms with a knife, saying " 'Tis for the love they bear to such a boy".'[11]

The young slave might also be in peril from the amorous attentions of his mistress. Pitts assures us that

> the Turks are but seldom jealous of their slaves, though 'tis thought oftentimes they are made cuckolds by them, and that by the sollicitations of the Patroonas or Mistresses themselves; for it would be dangerous presumption for the slave to dare to make the least item that way without encouragement from his mistress. I have heard of some who

have suffered much like Joseph for refusing to comply with the lascivious desires of their mistresses; who, like Potiphar's wife, have forg'd a quite contrary story to their husbands, which has occasioned the poor slave to be severely beaten, and afterwards to be sold.[12]

The law demanded in fact still more terrible penalties for sexual intercourse between a Christian man and a Moslem woman; the former to be beheaded or burned alive, the latter sewn up in a sack and thrown into the sea. Suspicion alone sometimes seems to have sufficed to draw down this terrible fate. At the end of the eighteenth century we have the case, recorded by a fellow-slave, of a woman discovered lurking in some bushes in the vicinity of a working party of beylik slaves. The Moslem guards, suspecting an assignation, seized her and were about to send her bound to the kadi when one of the slaves, in compassion at her probable fate, attempted to bribe the guards to release her. His intervention merely caused them to jump to the conclusion that he was the intended paramour. The kadi condemned them both to death. Shortly after they had been led away to execution, witnesses belatedly succeeded in convincing him of the man's innocence. The kadi sent a messenger who arrived just in time to have the beheading commuted to a bastinado, but was too late to save the woman, who had already been drowned. Four days later her body was washed up on the shore fresh and uncorrupted. This was taken as a miraculous vindication of her innocence. Her remains were interred near by, and her tomb soon became a shrine where pious Moslems resorted to pray.[13]

Despite these terrible penalties, several writers assure us that affairs between Moslem women and Christians were anything but uncommon. Many cases are certainly on record of widows marrying their ex-slaves, and d'Aranda asserts that some wives, in order to achieve their desires, would not scruple to get rid of their husbands by administering a slow poison, in the concoction of which they were reported to be dexterous, and that the law would not enquire too closely into the circumstances of such deaths. Father Haedo assures us that

mere fornication is not regarded as a sin, and so numerous

are the harlots (though brothels are supposedly not allowed)
that they themselves say that there is no woman in Algiers
who does not behave like a harlot, not only with the Turks
and Moors, but even with the Christians, whom they solicit
and take home without fear of death by being cast into the
sea, as the custom is.[14]

Laugier de Tassy declares that lascivious women sometimes
smuggled their Christian paramours, heavily disguised and
veiled like the female attendants, into the public baths—'the
retreat and pretext of libertinage', according to the ex-slave
Chastelet des Boys. Laugier relates, in particular, a celebrated
affair said to have occurred in the 1680s. Seremeth Effendi was
a former artillery general in the Ottoman army who had settled
in Algiers after being disfigured in the explosion of a powder
magazine. The accident had blown all the hair off his head,
left his nose blackened with powder and his face blistered all
over, with two large scars on either side of his mouth, so that
'it looked as if it had been sewn together'. A great womanizer in
happier days, Seremeth Effendi was not discouraged from
adding a beautiful twelve-year-old girl to his harem, but as he
was of enormous girth, as well as of repulsive appearance, he
could not consummate the marriage before being called away
on active service. In the course of time, the girl grew to
maturity and fell in love with a young slave whom she took
with her, with the connivance of the General's other wives, who
used also to introduce their lovers, into the public baths. When
the husband at length returned, the older wives maliciously
betrayed the younger woman's infidelity. Such was the in-
fatuation of Seremeth that he might have forgiven her even
this, had it not been discovered that the slave she had taken as a
lover was a Jew. For this there could be no pardon, and the
slave was condemned to the stake and the guilty wife to the
sack. Seremeth left Algiers with the intention of leading a
bachelor's life in the country; after he had gone it was discovered that he had also avenged himself on his four tell-tale
wives, whose bodies were found impaled in the cellars of his
house.[15]

Another tale of amorous intrigue in the public baths comes
from Sallee—less sensational, certainly, but perhaps hardly

less surprising when we remember the reputation that pirate lair had for its harsh treatment of the slaves. The Sieur Mouette, a Frenchman who spent many years as a slave in Morocco, related that de la Place, a young compatriot whom he knew well, was a great favourite with the ladies on account of his gallantry and skill as a musician. He gave lute and guitar lessons to the wife of the governor and other ladies, and used to accompany them every Friday to the baths. There,

> whilst they went into another separate bath, he remained with the other women who, quite naked, took their bath in front of him whilst he played the guitar to them, whilst waiting for his mistresses to fetch him. If anything more particular occurred during these gallanteries, I know nothing of it.[16]

Perhaps the scene becomes a little less incredible when we bear in mind the remarkable freedom with which the Christian slaves were commonly allowed to mix with and look on Moslem women, unveiled, in the privacy of their homes. Slaves were, after all, not human beings, but mere things; 'blind with the eyes of the body as well as those of the soul', as their mistresses would observe, not without a touch of coquetry.

The attractions of a liaison with a Moslem woman must have been all the greater since Christian slaves were discouraged from having relations with those of their own faith. To the resourceful, indeed, opportunities were never lacking. D'Aranda relates the case of a rogue priest called Domingo in Algiers who persuaded an avaricious old Moslem woman to buy a beautiful Christian slave on the assurance that he would raise a fat ransom for both of them, and he also promised the girl that he would marry her when they were freed; but the priest was penniless, and the old woman had to content herself with the addition to her slave establishment of the twin babes who were in due course born.[17] Breeding was not however generally encouraged—as amongst the Negroes of America—as a means of adding to the stock of slaves. Chastelet des Boys had the misfortune to be sold to a master who was an exception in this respect, and specialized in rearing mulattoes. For this purpose he kept a bevy of fifteen or sixteen Negresses on his farm outside

Algiers and periodically sent one of his white slaves in to them. The French captive was selected for duty and locked into the harem, with a supply of sweetmeats and fig brandy. He was fetched away six days later in a state of exhaustion and sold.[18]

The slave-owner's attitude towards his captives was conditioned by self-interest and by his assumptions regarding the natural place of slaves in Moslem society. Quite apart from Koranic injunctions to treat them humanely, he recognized that it was unwise to reduce their value, still more to cause their death, through maltreatment. Such considerations indeed scarcely applied to the beylik slaves who were regarded as expendable state property, to be exploited to the full for their immediate muscle power and then replaced by others from the inexhaustible harvest brought in by the *raïs*. But the private owner generally persecuted his slaves only in certain circumstances; to induce youths or women (whom it was regarded as shameful to take to bed unless they were Moslems) to abjure, or in punishment for some offence. The unfortunate Pitts recalls that

> within eight-and-forty hours after I was sold I tasted of their cruelty; for I had my tender Feet tied up, and beaten twenty or thirty blows for a beginning; and thus was I beaten for a considerable time, every two or three days, besides blows now and then, forty, fifty, sixty, at a time. My Executioner would fill his pipe and then he would at me again, and when weary stop again; and thus cruelly would he handle me till his Pipe was out. At other times he would hang me up back and heels, and treat me miserably. Sometimes he would hang me up by the armpits, beating me all over my body. And oftentimes hot brine was ordered, for me to put my feet in, after they were sore with beating, which put me to intolerable smart . . . I have oftentimes been beaten by my Patroon so violently on the Breech, that it hath been black all over, and very much swollen, and hard almost as a board; so much, that I have not been able to sit for a considerable time.[19]

The pipe-smoking bully had been hoping to flog the obstinate young slave into turning Moslem, but he eventually gave up and sold him to another master with whom Pitts managed to live 'very comfortably'.

The Barbary Moslem regarded his slaves as part of the natural order of things. He normally gave them the degree of care he would bestow on his ox or his ass to enable them to work adequately. He sometimes went further and accepted a faithful slave as a member, even a cherished member, of his household. If goaded beyond endurance, a desperate slave might turn on his master, even though he knew it would cost him his life. He might also be capable of astonishing loyalty. D'Aranda records two remarkable instances of this sort. A slave once found a diamond ring which he submissively took to his master Ali Piccinino, who merely called him a fool for parting with something with which he could have bought his freedom.[20] Another, a young Spaniard, was seized by corsairs whilst out fishing. His captor proved to be a Spanish renegade called Saban Gallan Agha, who hailed from the same locality and who released him on condition that the prisoner went back home and paid his ransom of 150 patagons to the Saban family. The fisherman did so, though he had to sell up his possessions to raise the money. No sooner was the transaction completed than the unfortunate man was again seized by corsairs who took him back to Algiers where he sent word to Saban Gallan Agha. His old master then bought him and sent him home once again on his promise to pay his ransom once more to the same family. As the fisherman had no possessions left of his own, he was given two years in which to discharge his debt, but by the end of that time he had raised only one-third of the sum required. With this he bought a consignment of tobacco, which he knew was in short supply in Algiers, and took ship to that port. There he sought out his old master and told him that if the sale of the tobacco brought him less than the balance of his ransom he would remain with the renegade as his slave. Saban Gallan Agha took him to his own house and after the goods had been sold sent him back to Spain with the proceeds.[21]

Such instances show that not all captives were corrupted by the squalid indignity of slavery and the constant struggle to survive. Father Haedo, though full of compassion for their sufferings, declares that immorality of every sort was rife amongst the slaves, most of whom were Christian only in name. He complains particularly of their thieving, drunkenness and profanity, and the callousness which led them 'to rejoice at the success and prosperity of the Turks and to jeer at the wretches who are brought in captive'.[22] For the slaves were enmeshed in a system which linked their own well-being with that of their captors and enemies. Craftsmen were given inducements to use their skills to the full in the corsairs' service. A master-ship-wright received a generous bread ration together with six to ten doblas a month, and other artisans were correspondingly rewarded. On the completion of a new warship, the slave-craftsmen were given a feast. Mast and rigging were bedecked with gay cloths which were then shared out amongst the slaves. Owners and captains brought presents for them, and as the ship glided into the sea, a sheep would be sacrificed and its carcass thrown overboard to stain the water red in token of the blood of the infidel which would soon be shed. Only men of exceptional moral toughness—such as the stout Protestant Richard Hasleton, who preferred the harsh anonymity of the galley-slave's bench to the status he would have gained as an experienced gunner (see p. 131)—persisted in concealing skills which would have been turned to account by the enemies of their faith.

Most slaves simply came to terms with their lot as best they could. For those fortunate enough to have a reasonable master and some means of livelihood, life could be made quite tolerable. They might gradually pay off the ransom agreed with their owners, and there were even those who seemed in no hurry to complete the deal and return home. But so long as they were slaves, their situation remained precarious, and they had to be careful to steer clear of trouble. Even to walk through the streets had its dangers, for they were so rough and narrow that there was scarcely room for two men to pass; a slave might be jostled by some quarrelsome Turk who could then threaten him with death by declaring that the Christian had raised his hand against him. This was particularly apt to happen in the late afternoon, when the bagnio taverns disgorged their drunken customers, and in Ramadan, when the tempers of men who had been fasting all day grew short; the prudent Christian would, if he could, avoid venturing out at such times. If he had the money and the leisure, however, he was free to enjoy such amenities as the city had to offer. Unlike the Jews, who had to wear the drabbest of clothes and were denied entrance to the public baths, he could make use of those institutions as freely as any Turk or Moor. He could visit the taverns or, on payment of a small fee to the Guardian Pasha, the chapels. He was required to wear the clothes prescribed for a Christian slave—a collarless shirt with wide cuffless sleeves, baggy trousers, and a close-fitting red felt cap—but he might choose them of superior quality.

The *élite* of the slave population was composed of those selected for the ruler's personal household. In Algiers, these fell into three categories. The lowliest, detailed to look after his gardens and the animals of his private menagerie, and to act as scavengers and porters, were not much better off than their fellows in the bagnios. The domestic slaves fared better; they were well fed from the Dey's kitchens, slept on reed mats, and had the use of the palace bath-house. A conscientious slave might attain the eminence of 'Chief Palace Sweeper', the highest post open to those in domestic service, or at least become one of the coffee-servers who had the right to expect the Dey's visitors to leave a gold coin or two in their empty cups. The richer and more important the guest, the larger the offerings expected. These would then be put into a special box in the apartment of the Dey, who generally added a contribution himself before dividing its contents twice a year amongst his domestics. These might amount to as much as 2–3,000 dollars. Slaves were entitled to complain, and often did, if the donations made by visitors fell short of expectations; was not this a slur on the august standing of their master?[23]

From amongst the ablest and best educated of his slaves the Dey would choose one to be his 'Chief Christian Secretary'. This was the most important post a slave could hold anywhere in his dominions, for matters pertaining not only to the slaves, but also to the Dey's dealings with European consuls and merchants normally passed through his hands. The Chief Christian Secretary accordingly wielded enormous influence, though the dangers to which he was exposed were correspondingly great. He was liable, like any other slave, to be arbitrarily beaten or even executed, specially if he brought unwelcome news or expressed unpalatable opinions. At the end of the eighteenth century this post was held by an American seaman called Cathcart whose linguistic talents, energy, unbounded self-confidence and successful operation of seven bagnio taverns had allowed him to purchase it for the sum of 1,383 Algerian sequins (about $2,500), half of which was loaned to him by the Dey.[24] Not the least of the Chief Christian Secretary's privileges (also that of the Chief Palace Sweeper) was the customary granting of priority for inclusion in any ransom deals.

The Beys who ruled the provinces composing the Regency sometimes also promoted Christian slaves to high office. A Frenchman called Thédenat, captured by the Algerians in 1779, was bought by the Bey of Mascara with the intention of making him *kasnadar*, chief minister and ruler of his household. For nearly two years this young man performed the dangerous responsibilities of his office, supervising the Bey's sixty servants, conveying tribute to Algiers, extricating himself dexterously from harem intrigues, intervening in favour of his less fortunate fellow-slaves, getting off with a mild reprimand after striking a Moslem with his scimitar, resisting inducements to turn Moslem himself, and finally securing his master's reluctant consent to buy his own freedom.[25]

Not all the cases of slaves raised to sudden eminence had such happy endings. In 1690 Louis XIV was surprised to receive a letter from Dey Cha'ban of Algiers informing him that, with the unanimous consent of the French community, a former merchant called René Lemaire, then a slave in Algiers, had been nominated acting consul. The king was not unnaturally reluctant to regularize the arrangement, but the Dey made it clear that he would not accept any other consular official. Lemaire soon proved himself an excellent choice. He vigorously defended French interests, attending meetings of the Divan with a copy of the current treaty in his pocket and insisting on securing its observance. He worked hard to mitigate the plight of the slaves and spent all he possessed in the process. 'I have passed all my youth here, in the dangers and tribulations you know', he later wrote to the Marseilles Chamber of Commerce, whose interest she served so well.

Three times they tied me to the cannon's mouth. Once I was taken out to be impaled, twice laid low by plague, forced, with my brother, to suffer the loss of 20,000 piastres; this would have been enough for anyone else to petition His Majesty for my recall. I have never set store on preserving my own life, but I have sought only to spend it in the service of the King and his subjects, and I console myself with the thought that, should I end up in the poor-house, he will have compassion on me.

The slave-consul did indeed die, as poor as he had once been in the bagnio, in the hospital at Marseilles. [26]

Slavery left its mark on the minds of many who regained their freedom. The grim nexus binding together captive and captor could not easily be broken. A Redemptionist Father returning from a mission to Tunis relates that he once reached Leghorn just as a ship-load of captured Moslems happened to be brought in. They were Tunisians, and amongst them the Christian ex-slaves recognized some who had until lately been their own masters. 'Your turn today; mine, perhaps, tomorrow'—the rough corsair saw had indeed been proven true. Some of the ex-captives jeered and gloated over this sudden turn of fortune. But others were filled with fear at the mere sight of their old masters. They could not yet believe that they were truly free. The victims had lost their chains, but their minds still bore the brand of slavery. [27]

5

Life in the Bagnios

No one quite knows how the slave-prisons came to acquire a name which, to modern readers, may conjure up a misleading picture of cool, marble-tiled Mediterranean bath-rooms. Most likely it originated, before the Barbary states became fully organized for slavery, with the practice of confining captives in the solidly built, vaulted bath-houses attached to most well-to-do Moslem households. At all events, by the early sixteenth century, if not before, the public or privately owned bagnio had become a grim feature of Tripoli, Tunis, Algiers and other places. In Morocco, captives were first kept in the even more inhuman *mazmorras* and were only transferred to bagnios above ground when they became too numerous for those repellent dungeons.

How large, then, was this Christian slave population? Sometimes the bagnios were full to overflowing, sometimes more than half empty, for the number of inmates varied with the ebb and flow of corsair fortunes. In the 1580s, according to Father Haedo's careful and detailed account, the slaves comprised more than one quarter of Algiers' 100,000 inhabitants.[1] Father Dan, half a century later, put it at much the same figure, with 7,000 in Tunis, a mere 4–500 at Tripoli, and 1,500 at Sallee, then beginning to take its toll of Atlantic shipping.[2] D'Aranda, a few years afterwards, estimates the number at Algiers as still higher—30–40,000, though other sources put it at only 8,000 (1650), 6,000 at Tunis (1651), and 1,559 at Tripoli (1671).[3] What is certain is that the eighteenth century saw a decline in corsair activity, with a consequent drop in the number of captives taken. In 1701, after their numbers had been thinned by plague, there were only 3,000 in Algiers, though the capture of Oran, half a dozen years later, brought in another 2,000. In 1749, Algiers was reported to have 7,000, but by 1767 the number had shrunk again to 2,662, and twenty years later, depleted by further ravages of plague and the effect of several large-scale redemptions, to a mere 500. But with the Napoleonic wars business picked up, and we hear of 1,700 slaves again in Algiers and 1,500 in Tunis.[4] When, in 1816, Lord Exmouth's cannon forced the reluctant Barbary rulers to acquiesce in the formal ending of Christian slavery, 3,000 were given their freedom. But old habits die hard, and by the time the French occupied Algiers fourteen years later, they found several hundred Christians still in bondage there.

How many Christians had had a harsh taste of Barbary slavery since the corsairs first began to ply their trade it is impossible to say. Dan, writing when it was still in full swing, estimates that the figure had already reached at least a million. This may well be an exaggeration; but we must bear in mind that the corsairs were interested in quick profits through a brisk turn-over of capture and ransom rather than permanent enslavement, and also that many of the renegades, who in the early days formed a large element in the population, had been enslaved before apostatizing.

The composition of the slave population, like its size, varied with the vicissitudes of war and the scale and direction of the corsair raids. In Morocco, it was made up largely of Spaniards and—particularly after the disaster of Alcázarquivir—of Portuguese; but by 1728, thanks to the activities of the Sallee Rovers, out of the 1,100 slaves reported to be in the capital, Meknes, 300 were English.[5] In Algiers, besides Portuguese and Spaniards, and still more in Tunis and Tripoli, Italians were plentiful as a result of the continual ravaging of the coasts of Calabria, Naples, Tuscany and many other parts of the peninsula. The larger Mediterranean islands such as Sicily, Sardinia, Corsica, Majorca and Minorca yielded similarly rich harvests. The south of France, despite treaty relations with the Barbary states, supplied a considerable quota, whilst Venetians and Greeks were brought from the eastern basin of the Mediterranean. Englishmen begin to figure from the time of Queen Elizabeth, and Americans from the end of the eighteenth century. Contingents swept up from far-off islands would make sudden appearances in the slave markets—Canary Islanders, after a raid on their homeland in 1586, Irish men, women and children from the fishing town of Baltimore in 1631, 800 from a swoop on Iceland in 1627. There were many Russians, much prized as galley-slaves on account of their strength, but described by d'Aranda as brutes who 'seem to have banished from their hearts, by some sort of natural antipathy, every sort of courtesy and civility'.[6] He describes a set-to in the Algiers bagnio between these Slavs and men from the Mediterranean countries which had to be quelled by Turkish soldiery. Riots too sometimes broke out between Spaniards and Portuguese, as when the latter wished to celebrate the recovery of their country's independence in 1640. Feuds could also occur within the same national group, as between the Bourbon and Austrian factions during the wars of the Spanish Succession. The huge, heterogeneous slave population, differing so widely in national origins and culture, and often rent by fierce political and religious differences, was thus almost totally without any feeling of solidarity. Despite their large numbers, any concerted action on the part of the slaves was consequently difficult to achieve.

One thing, however, which the slaves did have in common besides their chains was a language of a sort; the famous *lingua franca* of the Barbary Coast. This evolved in something of the same way as the natives and traders in the Far East evolved pidgin English. Basically an amalgam of Spanish and Italian, innocent of tenses, inflexions, or grammatical forms, its composition varied somewhat from area to area, having strong Portuguese elements in the western Maghrib, a more pronounced Italian flavour around Tunis, with a strong admixture of Greek as one proceeded east. Its simplicity and expressiveness, coupled with the fact that almost all families in the towns had their Christian slaves, whilst some were themselves of renegade origin, had taken Christian wives, or had traded with, and perhaps once been themselves enslaved to, Europeans, meant that it was very widely spoken and understood. It could also serve as the common tongue between Arabic- and Turkish-speakers. The Moslem had no need of linguistic subtleties for communicating with the Christians; a few clearly understood words of command and insults were generally enough, and further converse centred round the liberal use of certain key words and phrases. One of these was *usanza*, meaning tradition, the accepted order of things, 'rhyme and reason for every piratical, unjust and tyrannical act, for every unintelligible, strange and absurd custom'.[7] Another was *fantasia*, capable of many meanings, but particularly useful for indicating unacceptable opinions or conduct, or for discounting promises given or undertakings entered upon by oneself or another. *Mangiado* was another favourite, meaning literally 'eaten'—gone, lost beyond recall. A spendthrift's fortune was pronounced *mangiado*; a cargo or prize wrongfully seized and then reclaimed by an indignant consul was regrettably dismissed as *todo mangiado*.

Several captives have left descriptions of life in the bagnios, which seem to have resembled a cross between a Nazi concentration camp, an English debtors' prison, and a Soviet labour camp. Father Gracián, confined in a Tunisian bagnio in 1593, tells us that it was an underground dungeon, where 600 slaves were packed together like tiers of silk-worns waiting to hatch out; he was so heavily fettered that it was only with the greatest difficulty that he could stir from his bunk to celebrate mass at the altar he and another priest managed to rig up on the floor, and to preach to the other inmates from an empty barrel in place of a pulpit. By 1686 Tunis had nine bagnios, though the number had fallen to five by 1736. In Algiers, the largest of the prisons was the Beylik, or State Bagnio—a large rectangular compound nearly fifty paces long and twenty wide. A massive door opened on to a number of guard-rooms and antechambers hung with a collection of handcuffs and fetters of every size, which were clearly not displayed there just as ornaments. A vaulted passage led on to a spacious gravel courtyard flanked by stone arches supporting two tiers of broad balconies, behind which was a maze of small rooms rented out as sleeping-quarters to those who could afford them. The flat terraced roof contained a pent-house reserved for the most privileged of the slaves. In the dim recesses between the arches on the ground floor craftsmen had installed their workshops and tavern-keepers did a roaring trade during the day-time with Moors, janissaries, renegades and foreign seamen, as well as with their fellow-slaves. A chapel and a rudimentary hospital were in time added to the bagnio, as to many others. The Bagnio de Galera near the Marine Gate, and the Bagnio Sidi Hamouda, formed out of four ordinary houses, were built to a similar pattern though on a smaller scale.

Each bagnio was under the supervision of a keeper known

4 *left* Khair al-Din, known to the Christians as Barbarossa

5 *below* Algiers

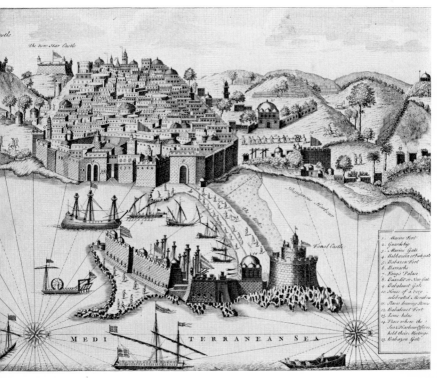

6 Torture and punishment of Christian slaves

as the Guardian Pasha, assisted by a guard composed of Moors and Turks and by a squad of 'corporals' promoted from the ranks of the slaves themselves. These men, who secured the privilege on payment of a fee to the Pasha, often tyrannized shamelessly over their fellows. They could punish offenders by chaining them by the leg or neck to a pillar at night, and, unless bribed off, would threaten to submit an unfavourable report which could earn their victim a bastinado. They also acted as receivers of goods stolen by the slaves which they disposed of in collusion with the guards.

The Guardian Pasha had powers of life and death over his charges. He might be a retired sea-captain or janissary, often easy-going so long as the slaves did everything required of them, but quick to treat the least sign of insubordination with the utmost savagery. Father Haedo tells of one Caur Ali, who cut off the head of a captive on the mere rumour that he was meditating a slave rising; this Caur Ali was a Valencian renegade who later became a corsair, was captured at Lepanto, and—in spite of his crimes—was pardoned and shipped off to Constantinople.[8] Ahmed, another Spanish renegade, who was in charge of the High Admiral's bagnio, was also reputed particularly severe towards his slaves. But though he made a show of driving them out to work with great brutality, he favoured them in secret, letting them slack off when no one was looking, and eventually seized a chance to escape himself when sent ashore with a landing-party on the Valencia coast.[9] In the early years of the nineteenth century, when humanity towards the slaves was no longer so exceptional, we read of a Guardian Pasha described as a 'superior person . . . , an ornament and honour to any country and creed'. This worthy, though a pious Moslem, became a close friend of the British consul and his family, with whom he spent many a quiet evening and 'took great delight in hearing stories out of the Old Testament translated to him'. He exempted old slaves from labour without exacting the customary bribes, and when the prisoners came back soaked from the winter storms, he 'would, at his own expense, bestow a glass of *agua ardiente* upon each of the poor dripping creatures'.[10] By an irony of fate, this benevolent Pasha was one of the first persons to be killed when Lord Exmouth bombarded Algiers in 1816.

The Guardian Pasha's responsibility for maintaining order also extended to all who patronized the taverns which opened in the mornings, after the slave-gangs had been marched out of the bagnios. Though alcohol is forbidden to the strict Moslem, the tavern-keepers did a profitable trade in the sale of wines and spirits, bought in the ordinary way of commerce and at the auctions of prize cargoes (and in Tunis, through the produce of local vineyards), as well as serving excellent meals. Many tavern-keepers were quickly able to earn enough to purchase their own freedom, though some 'abandon themselves to debauchery and libertinage and prefer to stay on in Algiers'.[11] But there were dangers too in their calling. Quarrels frequently broke out, and the law inflexibly ordained that any Christian who raised his hand against a Turk must die. Some tavern-keepers employed strong-arm men whose function it was to slip a ladder over the head of a boisterous Turk, imprisoning his arms between the rungs, and then quickly run him out of the bagnio where the Moslem guards would deal with him outside. Quarrels which resulted in deaths could have drastic consequences for the tavern-keepers as well as for the culprits. One wretched slave, goaded beyond endurance by the bullying corporals, went berserk and killed a couple of men before being overpowered and executed. The Dey declared that the brawl had been caused by drunkenness, and that the tavern-keepers must therefore pay the ransom price of the dead men. They were put in chains, bastinadoed, and their establishments closed, until they did so.[12]

On first arriving at the bagnio, each slave would have an iron ring riveted round his right ankle. This weighed a pound and a half, but it could be replaced by a lighter one, on payment of a prescribed fee to the Guardian Pasha and a smaller one to the blacksmith. Laugier, writing in the early eighteenth century, tells us that in Algiers fettering of the beylik slaves 'is generally disregarded, though the order is renewed from time to time, as there are sometimes old slaves who, familiar with the language of the country, dress in Turkish fashion and go out to do mischief in the Moors' farms'.[13] With the impetus given to slavery by the Napoleonic wars, the practice seems to have been more strictly enforced and the life of the bagnios more tightly organized. Foss, captured in 1793, described how he and his shipmates passed their first day in the Algiers bagnio. Sometime after incarceration, a French priest came to visit them and gave each a loaf of white bread—their first food of the day, since 'it is the custom not to allow the slaves any kind of food on the first day of their landing except a small loaf of bread at night'.[14] The new-comers had to file by a clerk, also a slave, who entered their names on a register. Each received a bundle containing a blanket, a *kaput*, 'a sort of jacket with a head', a waistcoat, a collarless shirt, a pair of trousers 'made somewhat like a woman's petticoat, but the bottom being sewed up, and two holes to put the legs through, and a pair of slippers'. A similar bundle, except for the blanket, was issued to the slaves once a year, on the Friday following Christmas day. The new slaves, wrapping themselves up as best they could in the blanket, dossed down on the bare floor until being woken up at about three in the morning and summoned to have their fetters put on. These turned out to be chains fastened to the leg and 'reaching to the shoulder and weighing about 25–30 lbs' (Plate 7). This was a far more formidable encumbrance than the token ring on the right leg referred to by earlier writers; perhaps the American captives had still to learn the miracles a well-placed bribe could do, or had not yet the means to provide one.

Beylik slaves not required for the galleys were assigned other heavy work, the most arduous being the hewing of great blocks of stone from the quarries a couple of miles from Algiers and transporting them to the mole which the winter storms rendered in constant need of repair. Blocks weighing never less than twenty tons were blasted out with gunpowder, manhandled onto sledges and down the hillside into barges from which the slaves had to hoist them into position on the mole. At least 500 slaves would be needed at a time for this back-breaking toil, and if the bagnios could not supply them, slaves in private ownership would be mobilized, generally on Friday, their purported day of rest. Overseers spurred on the gangs with sticks and rope-ends; accidents were frequent, and there were many cases of men slipping and being maimed or crushed to death under the huge rocks. In the intervals of labouring in the quarries, there was work to be done in the harbour; careening and fitting out the corsair ships, unloading the prize cargoes, cleaning out the harbour. The day's work, which had begun when the city gates were thrown open at dawn and the gangs marched out to their tasks, ended before sunset, when a white flag hoisted from the minarets signalled the faithful to prepare for prayers.

Some accounts speak of the slaves being dismissed earlier in the afternoon and left to their own devices until sunset, during which time they were expected to earn or steal their supper. Ali Piccinino, the High Admiral, never provided any food at all for those in his bagnio, and would observe ironically that 'they were unworthy of the name of slaves' if they failed to fend for themselves. Some of his captives proved apt pupils. D'Aranda awards the palm to an Italian called Fontimama who was once caught trying to sell the anchor of a ship he was helping to load, and coolly explained that he was doing so in order to lighten the vessel and let it sail faster; fortunately for him, the sardonic Piccinino was amused by his effrontery.[15] Though severely punished amongst Moslems, stealing was regarded as natural to a slave and seldom imputed to him as a crime. To break into the booths of the Bedestan merchants, or pilfer from the terraced roofs of the houses, was common practice. The Jews were particularly tempting targets, for a Christian knew he could insult or plunder them with impunity.

The daily rations doled out in the beylik bagnios were certainly too meagre to sustain hard physical labour. They consisted basically of two or three small loaves of coarse, sour-smelling bread, making a total weight of less than eleven ounces. Foss, writing when conditions had relatively improved, states that the first loaf was issued at about eight in the morning, when the men knocked off for a ten minutes' breakfast-break; the second did duty as the midday meal, when every eighth man also received a wooden bowl containing a pint of vinegar with which he and his fellows moistened their bread; the same ration—except for the bowl of vinegar—was issued for supper. Occasionally, as when the men were working on a corsair ship, they might be treated to a few olives or a little oil.

The situation was at once transformed if a slave had enough money to buy extra food or order a meal in the bagnio taverns. The universal aim was thus, by hook or by crook, to scrape together the means which would keep him above the level of utter destitution. A small fee paid to the Guardian Pasha would also entitle him to sleep in a bunk in one of the inner chambers instead of on the floor of the courtyard, and a larger one might excuse him altogether from forced labour. He was likely to be well placed to buy such privileges if he knew a craft which could be practised in a bagnio workshop, or—provided he returned to sleep there—even outside. The very fortunate lived on remittances from home or on loans advanced on the security of a promised ransom. The citizens of the newly emancipated United States of America appear to have been the first amongst the captives to receive regular, though modest, assistance from their government. When this became generally known, according to Foss, it made a great impression and caused the Algerians to exclaim that 'the American people must be the best in the world to be so humane and generous to their countrymen in slavery', and they declared that 'though we were slaves, we were gentlemen'.[16]

The profit motive provided as powerful a stimulus to life inside the prisons as it did outside. The *paga-lunars* were the *rentiers*, the tavern-keepers and craftsmen the successful entrepreneurs, of bagnio society. Those who could write offered their services to their illiterate fellows anxious to correspond about their ransoms. The corporals throve on their protection money, and there were others who acted as professional mediators and settlers of the frequent bagnio disputes. Some slaves carried loads of wood, or hawked water and trifles through the streets. The Muscovites, incapable of any more dignified work—d'Aranda tells us—were paid to clean out the prison latrines. A young German who had lost an arm when his ship was captured earned a living hiring out skittles to children. Nowhere did necessity prove a more prolific mother of invention; in short, as d'Aranda declared, 'there was no better university than the Bagnio at Algiers for learning how to live in the world'.[17]

Priests lived on the alms received in return for their spiritual ministrations. Though there were rascals, faint-hearts and even informers amongst them, as in every cross-section of slave society, many were men of saintly character whose courage and dedication invested them with extraordinary moral authority. We find Father Gracián, whose vocation had once been the contemplative life of the cloister, becoming the natural leader of 600 fellow slaves, to whom he acted as confessor, arbiter and general factotum. 'I reproved them, comforted them when they had been thrashed, tended them when sick, reconciled their quarrels, and when any one of them was in danger of having his ears and nose cropped, bribed the judges with money readily contributed by the Christians', he writes.[18] 'I kept their earnings for them, so that they might not gamble them away, . . . served as an oracle with regard to thefts, for if a Moor had had something stolen by a Christian, he would seek my help in recovering it.' Gracián wrote letters for the slaves about their ransoms, and exhorted those tempted to apostatize to stand firm. He even acted as a scribe for the renegades who came to him secretly with reports which they wished to smuggle out to the viceroys of Naples and Sicily—a dangerous exercise in espionage for which a fellow priest called Salvador de la Cruz was sent to the stake in Algiers shortly after Gracián had been ransomed. He also wrote certificates in Latin for renegades intending to defect, which they would then hide in the little pouches in use for keeping Koranic texts, so that they could prove to the Inquisitors that they returned of their own free will.

The influence of the priests was generally tolerated by their masters partly because Moslem rulers traditionally accepted the religious leaders of each *millet* or subject national community as its natural spokesmen, and partly because—as the Bey of Tunis observed of Father Gracián—they 'make my Christians good'. But slavery also threw up leaders whose authority stemmed from force of character alone. In the topsy-turvy world of the bagnios, rank and gentle birth ceased to command the respect elsewhere accorded them; they rather became liabilities which their possessors took pains to conceal from their avaricious owners. Quite other qualities were needed—fortitude, resourcefulness and unshakable faith—to lift men above the brutalizing effect of slavery and inspire others. Haedo recognized just such qualities in a certain young soldier, unknown as yet to literature, but already himself a man 'of whom a whole book could be written'. A fellow slave describes how, 'with the little he possessed, Miguel de Cervantes would relieve poor Christians, helping them to perform their daily tasks and live their lives . . . a man very discreet, of habits and tastes so good that all were glad to treat and speak with him, his society being sought by leading captives, both soldiers and priests, and withal amiable, courteous and open with all the world'. Another spoke of his 'worthy and Christian conduct . . . how he relieved poor Christians and kept up their spirits, comforting them in their afflictions and keeping them steadfast in their faith'. A new-comer declared how he had found in Cervantes 'both father and mother'.[19] All expressed admiration at the spirited answers he gave when questioned by Dey Hassan, a Venetian renegade notorious for ferocious cruelty, and his refusal to implicate others in his unsuccessful escape attempts—a miraculous triumph of genius and nobility of character over despotic power.

Without such gleams of humanity and more than human courage, the brutal degradation of the slave's life could bring him to despair. Suicides were not uncommon; Gracián records three such cases from Tripoli, where conditions were generally milder. Any activities which might bring hope and interest into the gloom of bagnio life were therefore of the greatest importance. The captives were generally allowed to celebrate the festivals of the Christian year. At the Moslem feast of Bayram, the Guardian Pasha and his charges would exchange presents; and though the Guardian naturally got the best of the bargain since each captive was expected to offer him a couple of fowls or their equivalent, his gift of a few sheep must have been very welcome. From time to time the slaves would stage their own dramatic performances. D'Aranda reports seeing one on the life of Belisarius, whose exploits in reconquering most of North Africa for Byzantium had clear political implications which must have delighted the audience. It is possible that Cervantes himself may have written pieces for the entertainment of his fellow slaves. The earliest of his extant comedies, written after his return to Spain, had Algiers as its setting, and he drew constantly on his African experiences in his later plays, his short stories, and for the lengthy Captive's Tale in *Don Quixote*.

The lot of the slaves was harshest in Morocco. Conditions there had once been much the same as in other parts of Barbary, where masters would buy and sell slaves in the knowledge that excessive ill-treatment would normally reduce their value. But under the long reign of Muley Ismael (1673–1727), Christian slaves became the personal monopoly of a despotic sultan who exploited them mercilessly to satisfy his building mania and rarely agreed to ransom them. In Morocco, as previously in Moslem Spain, slaves were customarily confined in *mazmorras*—subterranean prisons, which had often originally served as storage pits for grain. These were entered through a small opening closed by an iron grill, through which the urchins delighted to throw down mud and stones on the crowded inmates below. The slaves entered and left by means of a rope ladder which was drawn up after them at night. For beds they had reed mats which, in the damp and fetid air, stank so abominably that the atmosphere became insupportable; a few were fortunate enough to acquire goat- or sheepskins. The pits were generally circular, and the slaves dossed down at night, like the spokes of a wheel, with their feet pointing towards the centre, where just enough space was left for the urine bin.[20] D'Aranda, who was briefly imprisoned in a *mazmorra* at Tetuan with 170 Spaniards and Portuguese, found conditions there worse than anything he had known in Algiers. In Sallee, the roof of the largest *mazmorra* was supported by brick pillars and the slaves slept in tiers of hammocks suspended from the roof by cords. The floor of this prison was flooded for six months of the year; from time to time the cords would break and send a victim crashing down onto the sleepers below and into the water.

By the eighteenth century, when the slaves were concentrated at Meknes to labour for the sultan, they had become too numerous to be squeezed into the local *mazmorras*. They were set to work building a large walled compound, containing a number of mud huts grouped into four sections occupied respectively by the Spanish, Portuguese, French and English prisoners, each under a 'major-domo' elected by the slaves themselves. These head-slaves were exempt from forced labour and were under the supervision of a *qaid*, corresponding to the Guardian Pasha elsewhere in Barbary, nominated by the sultan. A few slaves whose services were regarded as specially useful—such as the chief jeweller to the queen—were allowed to live and work outside the compound.[21]

The tools and techniques used on the sultan's endless building projects were primitive in the extreme. The slaves made bricks in wooden moulds filled with moistened mud and lime, and had to carry the heavy loads up ladders whose rungs bit into their bare legs. Owing to the haste with which they were made to work, the foundations were seldom firmly enough laid, and walls would then collapse and bury slaves and passers-by beneath them. Sometimes, in an excess of fury, the sultan would order an unfortunate slave to be himself immured in the wall he was building, or he would send his soldiers to the top of the walls and order them to throw down the men who were working on them. His hand was seldom stayed by thought of financial loss; he took pleasure in the act of killing, and would often force his *qaids* and task-masters to repay him the value of the murdered slave on the pretext that if they had made him work properly the sultan would not have needed to put him to death. Sometimes the enormity of the task set them would cause a holocaust, as when 5,000 slaves had to extend the palace gardens by clearing the adjoining Christian graveyard, and 'fifty died by the stench of the bodies newly buried'. But generally the slaves would meet their fate by chance, one by one. Esprit d'André was caught stealing a piece of leather which he thought to sell in order to buy bread; he was castrated in the presence of the emperor and survived a further six years until, mistaken for another slave who had injured one of the royal dogs, he was thrown to the pack and literally torn to pieces. Muley Ismael

one day saw Jean Guéret of Brittany breathing a moment on the top of a wall; that merciless King immediately took up a fire-lock and shot him down, whereof he died on the spot. Abraham Lièvre died in the same manner. Marin Sally having committed the like fault . . . the King struck him twice with his spear and left him alive only because he thought him to have been dead. Jean Davias of Poitou, among strokes he received at his hands, had a cut which made his ear fall upon his neck, so that it hung by a thread; one of our slaves who was ransomed helped to sew it up.[22]

And so the catalogue of horrors goes on; the good Redemptionist Father who records them, and who undertook three not
very successful ransom missions to Morocco, reckons that
Muley Ismael was responsible for the death of 600 French
slaves alone, besides driving another 500 to apostatize. The
register of deaths kept by the Franciscans records the more
modest figure of 127 Christian slaves killed by the hand of the
sultan and specifies the mode of their execution.

Muley Ismael kept a menagerie of wild beasts and, like some
persecuting Roman emperor, would occasionally amuse himself by throwing malefactors or Christian slaves to his lions.
Mouette, who watched the whole scene through a peep-hole
in the wall of the slaves' compound, records one remarkable
event. Bernard Bauffet was a young Provençal whom the
emperor decided to make into a good Moslem. Five hundred
strokes of the bastinado and a lance thrust in the face having
failed to bring him to reason, the emperor ordered him to be
thrown to the lions. The hungry beasts made for him with a
roar, but then unaccountably sheered off. For five hours the
modern Daniel stayed unharmed in the lions' den, until the
keeper's wife, María de la Concepción, who had some influence
with the emperor and was always interceding on behalf of the
slaves, secured his release. The slaves who had witnessed their
comrade's ordeal were so impressed that they recorded it all in
a sworn statement and regarded it as frankly miraculous. But
the sultan had a more cynical explanation for the undoubted
fact of his slave's immunity. 'How repulsive indeed the flesh of
these Christians must be!' he would observe. 'Even the ravening
beasts refuse to touch it!'[23] Bauffet himself was later ransomed
but was soon back in Morocco acting as an interpreter for the
Mercedarian Fathers, to whose work for the slaves he resolved
to devote the rest of a life so providentially saved.[24]

In one respect, Muley Ismael seems to have shown himself
unexpectedly tolerant. Although the master of a huge harem—
he is credited with leaving at least 500 surviving male offspring
at the time of his death—the sultan refrained from adding to it
Christian women whom he knew to be already married. The
Franciscans were allowed to celebrate marriages amongst the
slaves—the proportion was about one woman to every hundred
men—and we know of at least one case of a reluctant captive,

who had no hope of being ransomed and no wish to father slave-children, being persuaded to take a twelve-year-old bride in order to save her from apostasy and the harem.[25]

Another concession which the sultan allowed his slaves was the manufacture and consumption of brandy. This came about in the following characteristic fashion. Impatient and surprised that the slaves were making such slow progress with his buildings, Muley Ismael was told that it was because Christians only worked well when given strong liquor to drink, as in their own country. He at once ordered a quantity of dried figs and grapes to be supplied by the Jewish merchants, and the theory was put to the test. After making and drinking this crude brandy, the slaves seemed definitely to be inspired with fresh vigour. The sultan thereupon decreed that they should continue to be well supplied, but that they should not sell their drink to Moslems. Despite this prohibition, some brandy was sold and the proceeds went to help finance a *cofradía* which the slaves formed amongst themselves for the purpose of relieving and assisting those of them who fell sick. Little could clearly be set aside for charity out of their own earnings; they received for their daily labour three small coins totalling about a quarter of a sou.[26]

The wild tribes of the coast and the remote interior did not always hand over to the sultan the Christian slaves—mostly victims of shipwreck—who happened to fall into their hands. Mouette speaks of seeing captives in the Sallee area yoked to a plough with asses and mules, and fed with the same fodder.[27] Few such unfortunates ever saw civilization again, but one Frenchman survived, against all odds, to return after thirty-four years of slavery and to give an account of his terrible experiences.[28] P.-J. Dumont, a Paris coachman's son, was born in 1768 and went to sea whilst still a lad. He was wrecked on the North African coast somewhere between Oran and Algiers, wounded and taken captive by the fierce Kabyles, and then marched inland to join the 2,000 slaves owned by a local Moroccan chieftain, Shaikh Osman. Except when accompanying his master on marauding expeditions, Dumont toiled at the plough. He went almost naked, but made a 'bonnet of leaves' to shield his head from the sun, and in time his matted beard grew long enough to cover his chest like a vest (Plate 8). The slaves were kept permanently chained together and were confined at night in a bagnio. When too old for work in the fields, they were employed inside this grim barn, sweeping up the filth, burning the vermin, and drawing water. 'These old men', he recalled,

> are more wretched than the other inmates, for in addition to their ill usage by the keepers, they are, as it were, the slaves of the other slaves who, driven by oppression almost to madness, wreak their vengeance on the old men, spitting in their faces, striking them, or pelting them with stones. When no longer able to work, they are shot, as are also such young men as fall sick, with but slender hope of recovery.[29]

The corpses of these discarded slaves were then thrown out and left to be devoured by the wild beasts, and their skulls were later collected and used as drinking vessels. Dumont adds that he used one such skull for fourteen years; 'from constant use it had taken the white polish of ivory—I used to drink my rum out of it on board the English frigate'.

Dumont owed his ultimate release to a series of extraordinary chances. Shaikh Osman planned an incursion into the domains of the Dey of Algiers. But a renegade Frenchman, who had been bastinadoed by the shaikh for peeping at the women of the harem, revenged himself by giving the Dey warning. The shaikh's forces were surprised and defeated and his sons captured. They would have been executed unless their father had managed to ransom them at the cost of handing over all his Christian slaves. Dumont was thus transferred to the relatively milder conditions of the Algiers bagnio where he remained until Lord Exmouth's bombardment forced the Dey to release all his enslaved Christians.

6

Escapes

Muley Ismael used to boast that he would drive his slaves so hard that they would not have the strength left to think of escaping and would lose the very remembrance of what it was like to be free. But men cannot stop dreaming of freedom, even when it seems hopelessly beyond their reach. They are for ever waiting for the wheel of fortune which has cast them into their present bondage to give another turn and set them free. And very rarely such a miracle would occur. The corsairs might be worsted in a fight and be chained to the benches from which their slaves had been freed; after Lepanto, 15,000 Christian captives regained their liberty. The slaves might sometimes even be able to strike a blow to hasten a Christian victory, as when, in the same year, the general of the Neapolitan galleys was in hot pursuit of Mehmet Bey, Barbarossa's grandson, bitterly hated by his slaves for his cruelty, and 'they fell upon that tyrant and had actually torn him piecemeal before the captors could possibly prevent such a piece of inhumanity'.[1] On land, the vision of a liberating Christian army haunted their imagination—a mirage indeed, for Algiers held out for three centuries against all attempts to take it. And when, in 1535, 12,000 slaves seized the citadel of Tunis from the janissaries, the Emperor Charles V's German troops indiscriminately slaughtered them for their pains.

Even without the prospect of external help, mass revolts or escapes were sometimes attempted, seldom without disastrous consequences. Concerted action needed a spirit of solidarity and resolution which the slaves were generally far from possessing. The conglomerate of wretches included too many who were passive, half-hearted or ready to betray their fellows out of spite or in the hope of some trifling reward. A typical case occurred in 1531 when Juan de Portuando, the high-spirited son of a Spanish general whose galleys had been worsted in a clash with the corsairs, found himself a captive, with half a dozen other Spanish captains, at Algiers. Portuando corresponded secretly with the governor of the *presidio* at Bougie who smuggled into the bagnio, amongst the provisions, a cask filled with swords. One Spanish slave made a set of false keys with which to open the prison doors; another, a gun-founder, 'cast them a huge iron mace with its chain, wherewith to break through barred and bolted gates'.[2] Whilst these preparations were secretly in progress, a dispute arose amongst the Spaniards at cards, involving a certain Francisco de Almanza—an untrustworthy rascal who had twice changed his religion and now passed for a Christian. The captains, called upon to arbitrate the case, found against de Almanza, who thereupon sneaked off and gave away the plot. Seventeen of the ringleaders were at once seized, and without more ado hustled away and hacked to death outside the city gates.

Some years later we hear of another attempt at a mass break-out organized by a Spaniard called Cuellar who 'had a strange and surprising faculty of running up and down any wall with the same ease as a rat'. Despite this useful accomplishment, he was caught, beaten to death, and the plot foiled.[3] In 1579 there followed a venture which proved at least partially successful. More than a hundred Christian slaves succeeded in overpowering their Turkish guards on a galley which had put in to Bône to take on provisions. They then escaped to Majorca, where about half their number fitted out a brigantine and made for Barcelona. On the way there they were intercepted by Algerian corsairs, and after a fierce fight their craft capsized and the ex-slaves were either drowned or recaptured. Three of the ringleaders were strung up by their feet from the yard arm. One of them managed to free himself 'and was found, two days later, in another galliot and pardoned'.[4]

One of the most remarkable mass escapes on record was organized by an English captive, John Fox from Woodbridge in Suffolk, who lived for fourteen years as a slave in Alexandria, where he worked as a barber and appeared quite resigned to his fate. Taking half a dozen of his compatriots into his confidence, and also a Spanish tavern-keeper who had been a slave for an even longer period, Fox at length procured a number of files and improvised weapons with which he killed the Guardian Pasha and his guards in a surprise attack. A galley was rapidly equipped and made off under fire from the port batteries. After twenty-eight days at sea, during which time eight men died of starvation, the fugitives reached Crete where they were given a hero's welcome by the monks of a Dominican monastery; 'they kept the sword wherewith John Fox had killed the Keeper, esteeming it a most precious jewel, and hanged it up for a monument'. Fox went on to Rome with a letter of commendation to the Pope who received him graciously, and then to Spain, where the king rewarded him by giving him a licence to beg alms and offered him a commission as a gunner. Fox does not appear to have taken up the offer, for by the end of the year we find him safely back in England. His achievement in organizing the successful escape of 258 Christian slaves, belonging to eleven different nationalities, and though himself a stout Protestant, leading them to safety, remains a remarkable achievement and an exercise in oecumenical militancy which must have few contemporary parallels.[5]

Attempts at mass escape continued sporadically throughout the seventeenth and eighteenth centuries, most of them ending tragically. In 1662 some Christian slaves in Algiers plotted an armed rising with the connivance of Moorish dissidents. It was savagely suppressed, and its leader, a Dominican friar, was tortured and impaled without divulging the names of his accomplices.[6] Early in the following century, the slaves succeeded in crawling through the sewers and out into the harbour where they seized a boat. The barking of the dogs raised the alarm and most were recaptured, though some got away safely to Majorca. We hear of a serious rising in the 1750s, when discipline had grown lax following the ravages of plague and famine, and the slaves broke down the bagnio gates and raged through the streets of Algiers, arms in hand, under the unlikely leadership of a Swiss clock-maker, before the rising was quelled.[7] In 1772 a successful escape occurred of which the Annual Register gives the following account:

A most remarkable escape has lately been effected here which will undoubtedly cause those that have not had that good fortune to be treated with the utmost rigour. On the

morning of 27 July, the Dey was informed that all the
Christian slaves had escaped overnight in a galley. This news
soon roused him, and it was found to have been a pre-
concerted plan. About 10 p.m. seventy-four slaves who had
found means to escape from their masters met in a large
square near the gate which opens to the harbour, and being
well armed, they soon forced the guard to submit, and to
prevent them raising the city confined them all in the
powder magazine. They then proceeded to the lower part
of the harbour, where they embarked on board a large
rowing polacre that was left there for the purpose and
passed both the forts. As soon as this was known three large
galleys were ordered out after them, but to no purpose.
They returned in three days with the news of seeing the
polacre sail into Barcelona, where the galleys durst not go
to attack her.

The same journal records the escape of forty-six captives
employed in a stone-quarry, who overpowered their guards
and the sailors of the boat which they were loading, took
possession of it, and managed to escape to Majorca. The
following year an attempt was made under the leadership of
an Italian called Trinquete to escape by night when all the
corsair ships in Algiers were beached for the winter. A dozen
slaves slipped away in a stolen boat and set course for Majorca.
After forty miles, however, an adverse wind drove them back
onto the African shore, where they were wrecked and recaptured, the ringleaders being beheaded and the rest bastinadoed.[8] The same pattern of attempted escape, recapture and
punishment was to repeat itself throughout the history of the
Barbary states. Foss recalls that shortly before his arrival in
Algiers, fourteen slaves had made off in a boat but had been
overtaken, the two ringleaders executed, and the rest sentenced
to 500 strokes of the bastinado. They were then made to work
wearing a 50-lb chain fastened to a leg at one end and a block
of wood weighing 70 lbs at the other; they were still kept in
this state when he left Algiers in July 1796.[9]
The normal treatment for offences meriting less than capital
punishment was the bastinado (Plate 6). This was not reserved
for runaway slaves alone, but was inflicted on all and sundry,

from unsuccessful or disobedient corsair captains and janissaries downwards. A few strokes would do little more damage
to the offender than a sound caning, but the generally savage
sentences of several hundred strokes would result in death or at
least many months of painful disablement. The English captive,
Okeley, gives the following description of the process:

> They have a strong staff about 6 feet long, in the middle
> whereof there are two holes bored into which a cord is put,
> and the ends of the cord fastened on one side the staff with
> knots, so that it makes a loop on the other side; into this
> both the feet of the person condemned to this punishment
> are put; then two lusty fellows, one at each end of the staff,
> lift it up in their arms, and twisting the staff about till the
> feet are fast pinched by the ankles, they raise the feet, with
> the soles upwards, as high as their shoulders, and in this
> posture they hold them, the poor man in the meantime
> resting only with his neck and shoulders on the ground. Then
> comes another knave behind him and with a tough short
> truncheon gives him as many violent blows on the soles of
> his feet as the Council shall order.[10]

The death penalty, invariably inflicted on the ringleaders of
slave-revolts or break-outs, and often for individual escape
attempts, as well as for a series of other offences such as sedition,
assaults on Turkish soldiers, insults to or apostasy from the
Moslem faith, serious theft or debt defaulting, and seduction of
Moslem women have been chronicled in macabre detail by
Fathers Haedo, Dan and many others. They are not untypical
of their age, including the gleeful excitement aroused by the
spectacle of public executions, though they were sometimes
meted out at the callous whim of a despot or with a barbarous
refinement of cruelty which Catholic Europe might find
unfamiliar and therefore shocking. Men condemned to be
burned alive—the fate reserved for Jews, lapsed Moslem converts, Catholic priests executed in reprisal, and other special
malefactors—were not just consumed on the top of a pile of
faggots but were secured to a stake in the centre of a ring of
small fires so that they were slowly and literally roasted alive.
Impalement was generally on the sharp turned-up spikes let

into the city wall, from the top of which victims were hurled down and left to die in whatever random position they happened to be transfixed. Crucifixion might take the form of a St Andrew's Cross or of being transfixed by knives to a doorway. Immurement in the city walls or brick cells, vivisection by sharp knives, and dragging at the tail of horse or mule were other methods. Morgan, the consular official and lively chronicler of the Algerian scene, who left his post in 1720, records that

> these terrible executions are not very frequent in Barbary, though there are others not much better, as may be hinted. All the time of my being there, I never heared of above three persons impaled, all which I saw . . . I likewise saw one man and one young woman dragged to death at mules' tails.[11]

Foss records that punishment of runaway slaves by crucifixion had grown less common, though he had himself often witnessed beheadings and bastinadoes.[12]

A few cases are on record of captives regaining their liberty by overpowering their captors on the high seas. This was particularly liable to happen in the early seventeenth century, before the corsairs had become accustomed to handling sail. A typical episode of this sort occurred in 1621 when Captain John Rawlins, master of a small Plymouth barque, was captured and incapacitated by an injury to his hand. He was bought by an English renegade, Henry Chandler, known to his fellow Moslems as Ramadan Raïs, and taken on as a pilot. The rest of the corsair's crew were a mixed bag of Turks, Dutch and English, some slaves and some renegades. When the ship had sailed out into the Atlantic, Rawlins won over the slaves and even persuaded the renegades to join in once the mutiny had started. The watchword 'God, King James, and St George for England!' was given and the Moslems, being outnumbered, were either killed or forced below hatches. Rawlins was able to take command of the ship and bring her into Plymouth with his captives. At about the same time, one or two other small vessels, which had been taken by the corsairs and their prize crews ordered to make for Algiers, managed to reach Penzance in safety. Incredible as it may seem, the Moslem corsairs were at this time so unfamiliar with navigating sailing craft in northern waters, that they were persuaded that the coast sighted was that of Barbary.[13]

What must surely be a unique case of prisoners overpowering their captors, since the former were unarmed and fervent believers in the virtues of non-violence, occurred when a British ship was taken by corsairs off Majorca in 1663. The mate, Thomas Lurting, was a stout Quaker who had great influence with the other members of the crew and persuaded them to offer the attackers no resistance. So they 'received them, as a man might his friends, and they were civil to us'. One night soon afterwards, when their captors were thoroughly off their guard, Lurting and his shipmates regained control of the vessel without striking a blow. Some were for killing the pirates there and then, or at least selling them in Majorca where they would have fetched a good price. But the Quaker insisted that they should be kept below hatches and returned unharmed to their own land. When they reached the North African coast, Lurting and a couple of friends, taking some of the ship's tools for their protection, rowed the Moslems ashore and left them, with some provisions and their arms, about fifty miles from Algiers. 'And with signs of great kindness, they took leave, and jumped out not very wet. . . . So we parted in great love, and stay'd until they had got up the hill, and they shook their caps at us, and we at them.' So ended this strangest of encounters between corsairs and Quaker pacifists.[14]

Spanish captives often pinned their hopes of escape on small craft sent over from Majorca or the mainland of Spain to pick them up at an agreed spot on the African coast. The difficulty here was largely one of timing; to assemble the runaway slaves at the rendezvous and at the pre-arranged hour was fraught with danger both for the slaves and for their rescuers, who were liable to fall into the hands of the enemy themselves. Father Haedo relates the typical case of a young Genoese called Morato who, before being ransomed, promised that he would return on an agreed day to rescue some of his comrades. He kept his word, entering Algiers in disguise and arranging with his friends to gather at a certain spot on the coast the following night. But the plot was discovered, Moslems took the place of the Christians, and Morato fell into an ambush, though the escape boat managed to make off. After being cruelly beaten, he was buried up to his shoulders in the sand and lanced to death.[15] Some rescue attempts nevertheless succeeded, and there were even daring spirits who made a profession of organizing the dangerous business. One of these was Juan Felipe Romano, who operated from Valencia at the end of the sixteenth century and made at least three successful landings on the Algerian coast. On his third trip he safely evacuated a party of thirty-two men, women and children.[16]

Many rescue attempts failed through a break-down in communications. When Oran was captured in 1707, four Knights of St John were amongst the many prisoners taken. Despairing of ever raising the huge ransom demanded of them, they laid plans to be picked up and taken to Majorca. Files were smuggled in to them, and when they had freed themselves from their chains they waited the whole night at the rendezvous, but no sign of their rescuers appeared. Knowing the fate reserved for runaway slaves, the knights threw themselves on the mercy of a charitable marabout who interceded for them with the Dey. They were sent back to prison and eventually released, after nearly ten years in captivity, on payment of a reduced ransom.[17] A fellow prisoner from Oran, who had to wait seventeen years for his release, made a vow that he would return to help others share in his fortune. On reaching Cartagena he procured a small boat, and returning to Algiers in Moorish disguise, managed to rescue five of his comrades.[18]

Probably the best known of the innumerable attempts, most of them unsuccessful, to take off Christian slaves by rescue-boat was that in which Miguel de Cervantes played a leading part. He had been captured, together with his brother Rodrigo and other soldiers, when on his way back to Spain from Italy in September 1575. His first attempt was made in the winter of the following year, when he set off overland for Oran, but was deserted by his Moorish guide and forced to turn back. He was fortunate in being punished only by being more heavily fettered and more closely confined. When Miguel's brother and other ransomed Spaniards returned home in August 1577 they brought with them secret correspondence from their comrades still in captivity. Father Haedo implies that this related to a plot, in which Cervantes was to be the leading spirit, for a general rising of the slaves, with assistance from Spain, and declares that 'if his success had corresponded to his courage, industry and strategems, Algiers would today have been Christian—for his aims stopped short at nothing less than that'.[19] The plan must have been judged too risky and ambitious, for we next hear of a more modest scheme to send a rescue-ship to an agreed spot some miles from Algiers to take off fugitives. Cervantes was the chief organizer at the African end. With the help of a Spanish slave working in a garden near the rendezvous, he hid fourteen or fifteen Spaniards in a cave, keeping them supplied with food through a go-between and allowing them to come out only after dark when no one was about. When, on the night of 28 September, the rescue-ship arrived as arranged, their numbers had risen to between forty and fifty. At first all seemed to be going well. The rescue-ship established contact, but then had to put out hurriedly to sea again as it had been spotted by Moorish fishermen. In the meantime, the Spanish renegade who had been keeping the captives supplied with food lost his nerve and decided to save his skin by giving them away. He went straight to the Dey who sent a posse of armed men to the cave. All the Spaniards in hiding were rounded up and the gardener who had been helping them was summarily executed.

Cervantes took the whole blame for the venture upon himself, refusing to name any of the other ringleaders, though he was threatened and personally interrogated by the Dey, who was looking for an excuse to implicate the Redemptionist Father then heading a ransom mission in Algiers and to confiscate all his funds. The episode convinced the Dey Hassan that, instead of an impecunious gentleman, Cervantes must really be an important personage from whom a large ransom might be extracted. So he bought him from his owner and kept him in irons in his own palace. Even there Cervantes did not weaken in his resolve to escape, and he bribed a Moor to take a message to the Spanish commander in Oran. The Moor was intercepted and impaled, and Cervantes sentenced to receive 2,000 strokes of the bastinado. This would have meant certain death, but influential friends seem to have interceded for him and the punishment was remitted. Soon the irrepressible Spaniard was concocting another scheme, this time with a Valencian merchant and a renegade who wished to return to Spain and regain favour by secretly embarking sixty Spanish captives. This plot was betrayed by a Dominican friar. No reason for the friar's perfidy is known beyond a probable desire to curry favour with his captors, though it has been surmised that he was envious of the prestige acquired by Cervantes and suspicious of the broad humanism of his Catholicism. Cervantes had gone into hiding when the plot was betrayed, but he gave himself up after the Dey proclaimed that anyone found sheltering him would be put to death. The round of threats and interrogation was renewed, but Cervantes stood firm in his resolve to take all blame upon himself. It was probably his calm courage in doing so which won him the admiration of certain Spanish renegades who stood in high favour with Hassan and again prevailed upon the Dey to spare his life. In the meantime, a great influx of Portuguese prisoners had begun to arrive in Algiers following the Moroccan victory at Alcázarquivir. This greatly reduced the ransom value of the Spanish captives and made their owners ready to sell them for what they could get. Though his repeated attempts to escape had failed, Cervantes thus at last regained his freedom through ransom (see p. 117).

Of the numerous attempts to reach a friendly shore by crossing the Mediterranean in an open boat, one has aroused the special curiosity of historians, less for its intrinsic interest than because its protagonist was a no less famous figure than Cervantes—the great French religious and social reformer St Vincent de Paul.[20] We know of the affair only through two letters written by the saint himself, then a young priest, to his protector, M. de Comet, in 1606 and 1607, to excuse himself for not having written to that gentleman for so long. He had been captured, he explains, by Algerian corsairs and after being sold to different masters, he had escaped with one of them—a French renegade who wished to become reconciled to the Church—after a 1,000-mile voyage in a small open boat from the Tunisian coast to Aigues Mortes. The letters contain many curious details about his captivity, such as the help he had been obliged to give in an alchemist's experiments, and how the hearts of the renegade and his wife had been moved on hearing him chant *By the Waters of Babylon* and the *Salve Regina*. When, half a century later, the letters were discovered in M. de Comet's archives, they caused the saint, who was then in his last years, acute embarrassment and distress. He destroyed the copies sent him and wanted to do the same with the originals. Was this out of humility—for his implied part in the conversion of the renegade and the improbability of the escape itself smacked strongly of the miraculous—or from shame at having once dabbled in the black arts? Or had the whole episode been simply a youthful fabrication? We shall probably never know. No corroboration of the alleged African experience has been found, nor did the saint ever mention it in any of his writings or recorded conversations. Yet the fact remains that the plight of the Barbary slaves was something which he had always much at heart, and for the alleviation of which, as we shall later see, he founded an important Congregation.

If there was no boat at hand to steal, the determined and resourceful escaper might, in the face of tremendous difficulties, attempt to build one of his own. A feat of this sort was successfully achieved by an Englishman, William Okeley, captured in 1639 when sailing off the Isle of Wight. Taken to Algiers, Okeley contracted with his owner to work outside the bagnios selling wine and hardware, and then as a weaver. With six other English captives he secretly began building a small boat in a cellar, putting it together from odd pieces of timber and covering it with canvas made watertight with pitch. When completed, the frail craft had then to be dismantled, smuggled out of the city piecemeal and reassembled. Oars were fashioned out of pipe-staves, and some scanty provisions collected. When launched, it was found that the boat could only take five, and two of the captives had to stay behind. After a voyage of only five days, though they suffered greatly from hunger and thirst, Okeley and his four companions reached Majorca, and thence returned to England (Plate 12).[21]

To build, launch and make off in a boat under the noses of their captors might appear an almost incredible achievement; it must, by contrast, have seemed tantalizingly and deceptively easy to the slaves to swim out to a European merchantman or ship-of-war anchored off shore. Such attempts were frequently made, to the fury of the slave-owners and often to the embarrassment of the ship's master. The French, whose generally friendly relations with Algiers made them frequent visitors, and later the British, were the fugitives' main targets. Generally, but not invariably, demands for their return were refused. In September 1673, for instance, a score of slaves reached the safety of French ships moored in the bay of Algiers, and when the Dey sent the French consul to arrange for their return, he deemed it more prudent to abandon his post and sail off with them back to France.[22] Nineteen years later we hear of a ship from Marseilles repatriating eight Turkish galley slaves, but returning with forty Christians smuggled aboard.[23] Where the fugitive was of a different nationality from the ship on which he sought refuge, complications were liable to arise. When two slaves, one of them English, escaped on board another ship sailing to Marseilles, the French consul agreed to pay a thousand livres in compensation for the Frenchman, but sent the Englishman back—'an action which must stigmatize the French with infamy'.[24] Only with great difficulty did the English consul manage to save his compatriot's life by getting the Dey to accept an indemnity. But British commanders could also act with a notable lack of humanity, perhaps out of misguided anxiety to keep on good terms with the Moslems. We hear of a Frenchman, a surgeon by profession, escaping as a stowaway on an English ship, but being sent back to Algiers by the captain, though he had been a Huguenot by religion, with a wife and family in London. The Dey was delighted by the captain's action and rewarded him with the gift of a horse; but the English sailors were indignant and declared that a subscription ought to have been raised to pay for the stowaway's ransom. The Frenchman was fortunate to get off with only seventy strokes of the bastinado, and was later ransomed by 'a right reverend prelate of our Church'.[25]

In general, however, British ships offered asylum to all runaway slaves, regardless of nationality, as we see from the incident recorded in John Baltharpe's doggerel epic celebrating the otherwise rather inglorious expedition which Sir T. Allen led against Algiers in 1669:[26]

Whilst we lay here, even at noonday,
A Portugall escapt away.
In garden of his Pateroone*
He was a-working about noone;
Our boat he seeing near the shoar,
He straightway did his work give o're,
And was resolved for to dye
Or gaine desired liberty.
Through press of Turkes and Moores he then
Did run with pruning knife in hand,
Most like a valiant man and stout,
And every way did lay about.
By means whereof he free did make
His passage, and we in him take.
Some fifty years of age was he
When thus he gained his liberty
And was eleven years a slave
Unto a Tagarene† base knave.

Where the slaves were numerous and determined enough, they might even make a get-away by seizing a boat belonging to some European power. In 1714 more than thirty slaves of various nationalities who were working in the harbour of Algiers seized an English merchantman, clapped the master and officers below hatches, and sailed off, defying the fire of the port batteries. A resolute Dutchman took charge, and held off their pursuers with the ship's cannons and muskets. The master and officers were released unharmed, and with apologies, when they reached Majorca; they returned to Algiers where the acting British consul and leading English merchants had been made to pay for the venture by a spell in the bagnio.[27] Some years later we hear of another case of the Dey avenging himself in still more drastic fashion on account of another attempted escape—this time unsuccessful. The master and three sailors from an English merchantman had come ashore, leaving only two seamen and a couple of boys on board. A group of eighteen Spanish captives were able to seize control and would have made off in the English vessel had they not run foul of an Algerian ship, when they were boarded and

* *Patrón*, master   † *Tagarín*, Morisco from Andalusia

overpowered. The English master managed to find asylum in the British consulate, but his ship was sacked and the sailors sent to labour in the bagnio on the pretext that they had been in league with the Spaniards. The latter were dealt with in customary fashion, four being beheaded, and the rest each receiving 5–800 strokes of the bastinado.[28]

If attempts to escape by sea sometimes succeeded as a result of determination and good luck, the overland route was virtually certain to lead to death or a still more unendurable servitude at the hands of the Kabyles. The fugitive's only hope was to reach one of the few Christian *presidios*, such as Oran on the Mediterranean coast, or Larache and Mamora on the Atlantic, which the Moslems kept closely invested. Even though a runaway slave might remain at large in the wilderness for a considerable period, this final leap to safety was generally his undoing. We hear of an adventurous Frenchman captured by Tripoli corsairs in 1672 who mastered Arabic speech and customs so thoroughly that he was able to survive for years as a wandering marabout and eventually reach Morocco with a pilgrim caravan; there, after soldiers had discovered that he was not circumcised, the impostor was apprehended, escaped again, and had almost reached the safety of Tangier when he was shot by a drunken Irish guard—whether fatally or not we do not know.[29]

As if these natural obstacles to freedom were not enough, Father Dan assures us that Moslem magicians worked hard to cast spells on the fugitives. He avers that Captain Matan of La Rochelle, whilst on the point of reaching the *presidio* of Mamora, was suddenly seized by diabolically induced stomach cramps which ceased as soon as he turned back, 'when he seemed to fly rather than to walk'. Other runaway slaves were stopped in their tracks by hallucinations; they suddenly fancied themselves confronted, the good Father tells us, by lions, tigers or armed men, or found themselves peering over the brink of a precipice.[30] But sometimes, the Christians firmly believed, supernatural intervention might favour the fugitive. In 1614 or 1615, we are told, two runaway slaves who were nearing the *presidio* of Mazagan perceived that they were being followed by a lion. Their fear turned to wonder when they found that the beast made no attempt to molest them, but would stop when they stopped, and seemed to be simply bent on scaring off their pursuers. When they were within sight of the *presidio* the beast disappeared and it was clear to them that they owed their deliverance to miraculous intervention.[31]

Many Christians would indeed have been prepared to make a pact with the Devil if this would gain them their liberty. Father Caronni, an Italian priest taken by corsairs in the early nineteenth century, related the following amusing conversation with his fellow captives after they had been landed from a lightly guarded ship and were waiting to be marched overland to Tunis:

'Father, say a prayer which will cast a spell on the guards for just a quarter of an hour, and we promise you that we shall all regain our freedom!'

'What, my children? Say a prayer to the Devil? That shall never be! Would you have a priest commit so great a sacrilege?'

'We would go and seek pardon for it in Rome.'

'And if the divine vengeance should overtake you before?'

'Ah Father, with such scruples you will remain a slave for the rest of your life!'[32]

In Morocco, despite the odds against reaching safety from the sultan's inland capital of Meknes, and the fearsome punishments meted out to those who were caught, desperate attempts to escape continued to be made—about twenty of them every year, according to Mouette.[33] He tells us that the best day to start was a Friday, when the Moslems were at their prayers. The fugitives, with their scanty provisions of dried bread, would be hidden by their comrades—a favourite spot was the ditch outside the castle at Meknes used by them as a latrine, for its stench discouraged detection—until nightfall when they would steal off, commending themselves to the Virgin and setting their course by the stars. Thomas Phelps, an Englishman captured in 1684, escaped in this way with three other Englishmen. Travelling by night and feeding on a diet of grain, pumpkins, snails and tortoise, they reached the coast at Sallee, sailing out in a stolen row-boat over the protective sandbank to reach a British man-of-war blockading the port. These intrepid men then volunteered to pilot a raiding party into the harbour, which they did, destroying two ships laid up there, one belonging to the corsair admiral and the other—'by the wonderful providence of God to whom vengeance belongeth'—the very vessel which had previously taken Phelps captive![34]

Sometimes the fugitives had the help of professional guides or *metedores*—daring men familiar with the country and friendly with the natives who traded with the *presidios*. Three Englishmen—Francis Brooks of Bristol, Tristan Bryan of Plymouth, and Edward Tucker from New England—reached Mazagan in 1692 with the help of a *metedor* who received a reward of forty pieces-of-eight from the governor, but was caught on leaving the *presidio* and sent to the stake.[35] Muley Ismael did his utmost to stamp out this dangerous trade by inflicting the most ferocious punishments. Runaway slaves were generally given the choice between apostasy and beheading, or at least received a merciless thrashing, but the *metedores* were subject to more refined tortures. We hear of two wretches who were left with their hands nailed to a door. One lingered on in agony for three days, the other tore himself free but was finished off by the onlookers.[36] On another occasion, the sultan had twenty-two persons executed on the spot on mere suspicion of having helped some *metedores*. The latter sometimes found it safer to double-cross their clients, robbing and abandoning them in the wilds. We hear of one slave avenging himself on the *metedores* in terrible fashion, and provoking the sultan to an orgy of indiscriminate slaughter. Two Moslems were denounced by a Christian informer in Sallee as *metedores*. When they were brought before him, the sultan ordered his Negro guards to execute them. This they did, but in so disorderly a fashion that balls discharged by their firearms grazed their master's head and leg. Turning his rage against the blacks, Muley Ismael slew three of them with his scimitar, had seven more strangled, and the remaining 400 heavily fettered and imprisoned. Twenty more subsequently died under the bastinado. Horrified at this holocaust, the Redemptionist Fathers wrote a letter of reproof to the Christian slave whose denunciation had been the cause of the tragedy.

'He made a scurvy excuse, alleging that what he had done was to avenge his brethren, whom the *metedores* often murder by the way, to rob them, instead of conducting them in their flight.'[37] The Redemptionists nevertheless regarded the *metedores* as generally trustworthy and continued to make use of their services. We find Father Busnot in touch with two of them in Cadiz and paying them 120 ducats a head for every fugitive safely conveyed out of Morocco to Málaga.

7
Renegades

To the slave who had no chance of escape and little hope of ransom, another door stood temptingly ajar. Apostasy seemed to offer him a way of bettering his lot, perhaps even of winning him fame and fortune. Though some entered upon this course heedlessly enough, it was a fateful step to take. The renegade turned his back on his home and family in the knowledge that he would probably never see them again. There, in the alien world of Islam, amongst the traditional foes of his faith and people, he would be given another name, don different clothes, acquire a new identity and profess a new allegiance. It would cost him, the Church warned, the loss of his immortal soul.

The welcome which Islam gave its converts had been a major source of its strength and a cause of its rapid expansion. The number of apostasies was undoubtedly very high; Gracián puts it in his day at one half at least, and perhaps as much as three-quarters, of all Christians taken captive.[1] In contrast to Catholic Spain, which discriminated against its 'new Christians' and hounded them through the Inquisition, converts to Islam were not regarded as second-class Moslems. We know of one, a Spaniard from Córdoba, who became a marabout hermit in the hills round Algiers, where his shrine continued to be much venerated; another, Sidi Butaybo, also won repute as a marabout, scholar, and diplomatic envoy.[2] Of the forty-eight grand viziers who held power in Constantinople between 1453 and 1623 at least thirty-three are known to have been of Christian origin.[3] In Barbary, during the sixteenth and seventeenth centuries, this pre-eminence was even more marked. The great Khair al-Din chose renegades for his personal bodyguard and used them when necessary to quell his mutinous janissaries. Many who followed him as rulers of Algiers were renegades: his favourite and successor, Hassan Sardo, who routed the Emperor Charles V's expedition and has been described by a sympathetic chronicler as 'the very best Governor Algiers ever had'; Hassan Corso, 'a most worthy personage, exceedingly mild, affable and liberal, and so far from being an enemy to the Christians that he bore a very singular affection to them and their concerns'—one reason, perhaps, why his short rule ended in mutiny and impalement; the Calabrian al-Qaid Yusuf, 'excessively courteous and obliging'; the great 'Eulj 'Ali (Ochiali), once nicknamed Fartax or 'Scabby' on account of the scurvy contracted whilst a Christian galley-slave before apostatizing—'purely to have the opportunity of retaliating a blow'—and starting a career which was to make him ruler of Algiers, a renowed *raïs* and finally admiral of the Sultan's fleet; Ramadan Sardo, once a Sardinian goatherd, 'very prudent, upright, mild, humane and good-natured'; Ja'far Agha, a renegade from Hungary, described as 'excessively humane' towards his Christian slaves, insisting that they be well fed and clothed and only to be beaten at his express command; Hassan Veneziano, notorious on the other hand for his callousness, greed and ferocious cruelty.[4]

The early rulers of Barbary, whether or not themselves renegades, relied heavily on the latter as administrators and corsair captains. Of the twenty-three Algerine *qaids*—governors or high officials—listed by Haedo in the 1580s, more than half were renegades (including one Englishman); of the thirty-three leading *raïs*, twenty-five appear to be renegades or the sons of renegades.[5] According to a Spanish report of 1568, there were about 10,000 renegades in Algiers, two-fifths of them Corsicans.[6] Haedo says that they outnumbered the other national communities—Turks, Moors and Jews—and puts their strength at some 6,000 households.[7] 'There is no nation in the world without its renegades there', he declares; besides men from all parts of Spain, Italy, and Greece, he mentions Russians, Poles, Bulgars, Hungarians, Albanians, Germans, French, Scottish, English, Danes, Mexicans, Brazilians, Indians and 'Abyssinians of Prester John'. Father Dan, writing some fifty years later, puts their number at 8,000 men and 1,200 women for Algiers, 3–4,000 men and 6–700 women for Tunis, and about 100 in Tripoli.[8] For Morocco, numbers are more difficult to estimate. They would rise dramatically after the capture of a *presidio*; by the end of the seventeenth century, only 400 out of the 1,800 taken at Larache were still Christians, and of the 2,000 who formerly garrisoned Mamora, 'very few' had not abjured. Muley Ismael used many renegades in his armed forces, despite their unreliability. Following an attempt on his life by one of them, 1,500 were transferred to the remote province of Draa, which became known on that account as the Land of the Apostates.[9]

How many of those who renounced Christianity did so voluntarily, how many because they were forced? Our difficulty in reaching any conclusions is increased by the tendency of the Redemptionist Fathers to play down a phenomenon which raised disturbing doubts about the solidity of Europe's Christian foundations. Whilst Rome was fighting to stem the Protestant tide in the north, a flow of deserters continued to leave for the Moslem lands to the south. Many were simple seamen, peasants, artisans, prepared to 'turn Turk' in expectation of a better life. Boatloads of volunteers were constantly arriving from Sicily and Corsica. We even hear of Christian slaves, after they had been ransomed, deciding to apostatize, or—like the French writer Thomas d'Arcos, captured in 1625 and released soon afterwards—returning to settle permanently in Barbary.[10] Pitts refers to an Englishman of his acquaintance

> who had endured many years of slavery, and after he was ransomed and went home to his own country, came again to Algier and voluntarily, without the least force used towards him, became a Mahammetan. Another Englishman I knew, who was bred to the trade of a gunsmith, who after he was ransomed and only waited for his passage, reneged and chose rather to be a Mahammetan than to return to his own country.[11]

Other defectors were adventurers or criminals whose escapades had made Europe too hot for them. Perhaps some exaggerated their past misdeeds in order to cut a more romantic figure, like the renegade Spaniard, 'gay and handsome, but proud and ferocious', who spoke 'with a sanguinary exultation of the dreadful revenge he procured for himself' before seeking refuge in Tripoli. 'Hammed' claimed to be in reality the Marquis San Juan, a former guards officer from Naples, whose high-born wife had been seduced in his absence by the prince of Calabria. Surprising the lovers together, the Spaniard slew his wife with the sword, whilst the prince escaped through a window, and their bastard son was killed in the confusion.[12] Not all defectors could be assured of finding a welcome amongst the Moslems. Mouette tells of two young Spaniards cross-examined on their arrival in Tetuan. One declared that he wished to become a Moslem and 'renounce his country, family, friends and God'. The governor, enraged at the suggestion that the Moslems were a godless people, promptly had him executed. His companion, who gave the more prudent answer that he had tired of living under 'the false law of the Christians', was accepted, turned corsair, and later died at the stake in Seville after attempting to carry off his parents into Moroccan slavery to satisfy a whim of his Moslem mistress.[13]

But there were also captives prepared to face torture and execution rather than renounce their faith. In Morocco, Muley Ismael would sometimes confront his slaves with a stark choice between apostasy or death. Once, after having two slaves bastinadoed for alleged indolence, he thrust his spear against the breast of each in turn and called on them to declare themselves Moslems or die. The first abjured and was spared; the second answered that he would die a Christian. The sultan thereupon dropped his spear, merely observing—'Then this dog of a Christian will be damned!'[14] Such happened, on this occasion, to be the whim of the capricious sultan; generally the summons to apostatize or die was no empty threat. Often, however, more subtle inducements would be used. We have already noted what Haedo (and he is by no means alone) has to say about the Moors and Turks' fondness for young boys and how quickly they would corrupt them. Obdurate youths, as we know from the experience of Pitts (see p. 47), would generally be reduced by systematic beating. More fearful still was the maltreatment meted out by a Moroccan prince to young Thomas Pellow who, according to his fellow captives, 'endured enough to have killed seven men before his master could make him turn';[15] according to his own account, it was only after being starved, beaten and tortured—'burning my flesh off my bones by fire'— and even then he acquiesced 'calling upon God to forgive me, who knows that I never gave the consent of my heart, though

I seemingly yielded, by holding up my finger—and that I always abominated them and their accursed principle of Mahometism'.[16] After his apostasy a convert could usually expect very different treatment. A Moslem might become the protector of numerous renegades, formerly his slaves, whom he would treat like adopted sons, bequeathing his property to them if he died without heirs.

Moslem women sometimes bribed their favourite slaves to abjure with generous offers of money. Widows had no scruples about marrying them, and young girls were sometimes offered as brides, since their fathers would welcome a potential corsair or janissary into their households as a means of protection and possible source of profit. Father Gracián records that a priest held prisoner in Tunis was offered a dowry of 12,000 escudos if he would turn Moslem and marry a Moor's pretty fifteen-year-old daughter. Christian girls were in special danger of being forced into apostasy unless they were in a position to command rich ransoms. Gracián describes coming across a batch of Corsican and Calabrian girls who had just been taken captive. On making enquiries soon afterwards, he learned that all had already apostatized.[17] To resist absorption into the harem was a forlorn hope. Brooks relates the typical case of an English girl, one of four women taken by Sallee Rovers in 1685, who was sent to Muley Ismael for the honour of being deflowered. She resisted his persuasions to turn Moslem and capitulated only after being handed over to the sultan's Negresses who whipped her and tormented her with needles; 'so he had her washed and clothed her in their fashion of apparel and lay with her; having his desire fulfilled, he inhumanly, in great haste, forced her away out of his presence; and she being with child, he sent her by his eunuchs to Meknes to the Chief Eunuch, after that she was delivered of two children'.[18] Another Englishwoman is said to have had the good fortune to retain the sultan's favour much longer and to have been helpful to the Redemptionist Fathers.[19] No such kindly feelings seem to have animated the young English renegade who married an elderly Dey of Algiers in the seventeenth century; we find her described as 'a cunning covetous Englishwoman who would sell her soul for a bribe'.[20]

The act of apostasy could hardly be simpler. The intending

convert had only to declare 'There is no God but God, and Mahomet is his prophet'—even merely to raise his finger to signify belief in the oneness of God. The European powers were later able to insist he should first register his intended change of faith at a consulate. If he was a person of consequence, his adhesion to Islam would be celebrated with great pomp. The convert would be driven around in an open carriage, accompanied by a guard of honour with drawn scimitars. The Dey might present him with a costly caftan, and a bowl would be handed round in the mosques into which the faithful would drop generous alms, for it was a meritorious act to help set up a convert to Islam in honourable style. Humbler recruits were accepted with less ado, but still with a certain formality. A master would assemble his friends in his house and in their presence ask the slave if he wished to become a Moslem. The slave would reply by raising his forefinger and pronouncing the required formula. His hair would then be cut, leaving a tuft on the top in Moslem style, his cap thrown to the ground, and a turban placed on his head. He would assume a Moslem name, generally coupled with an epithet indicating his origin or office; Hassan Veneziano, Suleiman Raïs, etc. Dinner would be served, at which the apostate would be given place of honour. A surgeon would then appear and the act of circumcision be performed, after which the renegade might need to keep to his bed for a couple of weeks. This completed the conversion formalities. His fellow Moslems bothered little about instructing him in the new faith, provided he conformed outwardly.

Apostasy did not automatically set a slave free. 'I have known some that have continued slaves many years after they have turned Turks—nay, some even to their dying day', Pitts tells us. 'And many, I know, have been as little respected by their Patroons after the changing of their religion (or less) as before. For my part, I remained several years a slave after my defection, and suffered a great deal of cruel usage, and then was sold again.'[21] But though he might be denied his freedom, the renegade could no longer be fettered or sent to row in a galley. The corsairs, however, needed galley-slaves and were accordingly loth to let their Christians turn Moslem. So whilst certain categories would be cajoled or persecuted into apostatizing—boys likely to make good soldiers or seamen, skilled

artisans and technicians, beautiful women destined for the
harem, commanders, priests and other distinguished figures
whose conversion would confer prestige—the rank and file
would often be forcibly discouraged. Many must have been
tempted to behave like Ali Piccinino's French slave who, after
repeatedly being refused permission to turn Moslem, tried to
pass himself off as one by assuming Moslem dress and hair-style
and calling himself Mustafa. His master saw through the
pretence and ordered him to be beaten until he started calling
out 'I am not Mustafa but Jean!'[22] In this way the sardonic
Italian renegade could claim that he had flogged one of
Christendom's erring sheep back into the fold. As late as 1774
we find a Christian slave who was taking part in a procession
grabbing hold of the Standard of Islam and calling out that
he wished to become a Moslem; in spite of the crowd's
applause, the Dey had him taken back to the bagnio and
bastinadoed until he changed his tune.[23]

Father Gracián recalls an episode from his days in the
Tunisian bagnio which reveals the cynical attitude often taken
by the Moslem rulers in cases of this sort.[24] Mami, a Spanish
renegade, was incarcerated with the slaves on suspicion of
having murdered his master. Gracián, whilst taking some
lessons in Arabic from him, induced the renegade to seek
reconciliation with the Church and renounce Islam. Both men
were well aware of the cost they were likely to pay for this
desperate decision. Before the priest could give him absolution
and let him resume his Christian name of Alonso de la Cruz,
Mami had to recant and make a public profession of faith. This
he did in the forecourt of the bagnio, in the presence of
Christian and Moslem witnesses. The same night the two men
were summoned into the presence of half a dozen grave
Moslems, and their chains were struck off. This they took to be
a preliminary to execution, for condemned men were taken
out unshackled to their death. But they soon found that it was
only to have heavier chains substituted, Gracián being fettered
with a set the like of which was not to be found in all Barbary;
it had been specially sent from Constantinople for a Spanish
captain called Juan Valiente, 'whose deeds matched his name',
and weighed so much that the priest had to be carried back to
his bunk by his fellow slaves. He was not, after all, to be

executed, for the Bey had no intention of losing the huge ransom he expected to get for him. Nor did that cynical ruler want to miss the chance of gaining another slave for his galleys. 'Would that more renegades like Alonso, who are serving private masters, should turn Christian again!' he is reported to have exclaimed. 'Then I could use them for my galleys, as I will use Mami. It is punishment enough to spend the rest of one's life at the oar. But mind no one tells the Mufti or the Kadi, as we don't want our Papaz* burned. If anyone breathes a word I will have his head cut off, and that is the end of the matter.'

The usual punishment for a recanting renegade, as it was for a lapsed heretic in Catholic Europe, was death at the stake. Sometimes the martyrdom was involuntary, like that of the Frenchman executed at Sallee in 1634, who had previously turned Moslem, escaped to France, and gone to sea again, only to be recaptured and recognized by the corsairs.[25] Often it was a deliberate choice, such as that recorded, also at Sallee, of a Neapolitan captain who, having apostatized and recanted soon afterwards, was burned alive 'after having fervently received absolution and communion at the hands of a missionary disguised in the habit of a slave'.[26] Several instances are on record of priests who apostatized but later purged their sin by heroic endurance of torture and death. The French captive, Chastelet des Boys, one of those ordered to gather wood for the fire, tells us of Father Domingo, an Augustinian friar who apostatized, recanted, and suffered three deaths in one, being simultaneously strangled, stoned and burned alive.[27] Fray José, a pleasure-loving Dominican, at first secured good treatment by promising a ransom of 6,000 ducats which he knew could never be raised, apostatized when his deceit was discovered, but was reconverted by his fellow priests and died heroically at the stake.[28] Haedo, Dan and the other clerical historians include many such cases in their roll-call of martyrs.

There was little the European powers could do to staunch this running sore of constant defections, forced or voluntary, to Islam. A renegade could not be redeemed by ransom. A rare, perhaps unique exception to this rule occurred in 1605 when

* Priest

de Brèves, the French ambassador to Constantinople, used his influence with the Grand Signior to induce the Bey of Tunis to agree to release all captured Frenchmen (Plate 11), both Christian slaves and those who had been forced to turn Moslem. The renegades were permitted to return to France if they so wished, despite the rumours spread around by the subtle Tunisians to the effect that the announcement was merely a ruse to discover who were the true converts to Islam, and that those who opted to return would be sent to the stake.[29]

The official attitude of the Church towards its lost sheep oscillated between severity and clemency. The issue had been a controversial one in North Africa from the earliest times, when Christians had been required by the Roman state to sacrifice to the pagan gods, and a bitter schism had been provoked by controversy on how to deal with the *lapsi* who had consented to this. It reappeared in acute form as the Reconquest advanced in Spain, and the Church had to decide on its attitude towards those who had apostatized to Islam. Whether they were treated with leniency or harshness became largely a matter of political expediency. When Málaga, for instance, rejected the summons of the Catholic Monarchs to capitulate, captured renegades were mercilessly lanced to death. The lesson was not lost on Granada, which included large numbers of Moslemized Christians known as *Elches*, who were promised liberal treatment in the Capitulations. These included a pledge that

> no person will be allowed to maltreat, either by word or deed, the Catholic men and women who, before these Capitulations, may have turned Moors; if any Moor has a woman renegade for wife, she will not be pressed to become a Christian against her will, but shall be questioned in the presence of Moors and Christians and treated according to her wishes; and the same will be done with regard to the children born from unions between Christian mothers and Moorish fathers.[30]

So the *Elches* were at first spared the attentions of the Inquisition and lived on unmolested in Granada. But soon harsher counsels prevailed. Pressure, which the Church deemed 'persuasion' and the Moslems 'force', and thus a breach of the Capitulations, was applied against them and contributed to the resentment which drove the Moriscos to rebellion.

Opinion remained divided within the Church as to the wisdom of applying draconian penalties against captured renegades. Among the 'hard-liners' were the Knights of Malta, who constantly urged the Pope to approve sterner measures and stressed the unreliability of allegedly contrite renegades and the damage they might inflict on Christendom. They could point to the instance of Nicolò Rodiotto, who returned to Malta proclaiming a change of heart, but spent his time acquiring an intimate knowledge of the island's defences and approaches, and then escaped to Barbary where he organized raids and proved an adept at intercepting the grain-ships destined for Malta.[31] There were those, on the other hand, who advocated a general amnesty and pardon to all the erring sons of the Church as the only remedy.[32]

A genuinely repentant renegade could indeed perform useful service by turning his mastery of corsair tactics against his old associates. Cases occurred like that of the Sardinian renegade, Ciuffo, who in 1773 secretly negotiated a promise of pardon and allowed himself to be taken by the Christians in a feint raid. The islanders would have lynched him on the spot, but the authorities sent him away under guard to a monastery where he remained until the popular clamour for his execution had died down. He was then released, helped to organize the local defences, and was finally given command of a ship for operations against the corsairs.[33] But who was to know where the loyalties of such adventurers and opportunists, moving in the murky twilight world between Islam and Christianity, really lay? Take the case of the Corsican Sebastian Paulo, alias Morat Raïs. Some time after turning Moslem he escaped to Oran and reverted to his native faith, only to abjure again when he was taken prisoner and managed to convince his captors that he had always remained a Moslem at heart. He then resumed his life as a corsair. When the Christian slaves on board mutinied he persuaded them to let him return with them to Spain. There Paulo—as he once more called himself—was pardoned and taken to Court, where his ingratiating ways and his skill in using a Turkish bow won him much favour.

But after a time, he began to hanker after his old life and attempted, with some other ex-renegades, to make his way back to Barbary. He was caught and this time paid for his duplicity with his head, which was publicly displayed as a warning to all turn-coats.[34]

The Inquisition might discourage heresy through the terror inspired by an *auto-da-fé*, but it was powerless to prevent apostasies by a similar show of severity. The Moslems retaliated by burning not only their lapsed converts, but also perfectly innocent men, preferably priests, in reprisal for real or rumoured executions by the Catholics. Father Gracián relates, with his customary self-mockery, how he was all but awarded the crown of martyrdom following a report that fifty renegades had been put to death in Spain. Since the ship in which he had been captured belonged to the Inquisition, his captors assumed that he himself was an official of the Holy Office, and therefore a fitting object for revenge. Whilst waiting in the bagnio for the expected summons, Gracián was approached by a fellow slave who confided that he had a renegade friend who would creep up as the victim was led away to the stake and despatch him with a dagger thrust; for this merciful deed, an advance payment of ten escudos was demanded. Fortunately the Bey, reluctant as ever to forego the chance of a large ransom for his important captive, managed to resist demands for his execution until the clamour died down and the report—which proved a mere rumour—was forgotten.[35]

Renegades setting out on corsair raids were naturally aware of the fate they might expect if they fell into the hands of the Christians. Some accordingly sought to reinsure themselves by secretly taking with them papers attesting their orthodoxy. Gracián tells us that he made out many such certificates. Cervantes, who became familiar with the practice when he was in Algiers and saw how it was often abused, makes his Captive tell Don Quixote:

Renegades who have thoughts of returning to their own country used to get certificates from such persons of quality as are slaves in Barbary, in which they make a sort of affidavit, that such a one, a renegade, is an honest man, and has always been kind to the Christians, and has a mind to make his escape on the first occasion. Some there are who procure these certificates with an honest design, and remain amongst Christians as long as they live; but others get them on purpose to make use of them when they go a-pirating on the Christian shores; for then, if they are shipwrecked or taken, they show these certificates and say that thereby may be seen the intention with which they came to be in the Turks' company; to wit, to get opportunity of returning to Christendom. By this means they escape the first fury of the Christians, and are seemingly reconciled to the Church without being hurt; afterwards they take their time and return to Barbary to be what they were before. One of these renegades was my friend, and he had certificates from us all, by which we gave him much commendation; but if the Moors had caught him with these papers they would have burned him alive.[36]

Other renegades salved their consciences by continuing to practise their old religion as far as they were able, whilst outwardly conforming to the new faith. We find them paying furtive visits to the priests, mumbling a paternoster or an Ave Maria when at their devotions in the mosques, and making death-bed repentances, specially in times of plague. Many kept up family or business connections with Europe, sending gifts of money back to their relatives at home and acting as middlemen in the ransoming of captives.[37] Even a heartless villain like Morat Raïs—the Dutchman Jan Janssen—ravisher of the hapless captives from Iceland and Ireland, would stop in Holland to reprovision and see his wife and children, and in his old age, tried fruitlessly to persuade his Dutch daughter to live with him in Morocco.[38] So strong was the umbilical cord which still linked Christian Europe with even her most unnatural children.

Despite this occasional fraternization, there can be no doubt that the activities of the renegades inflicted immeasurable harm on Christendom. The defectors were not sheep who had wandered harmlessly astray, but sheep transformed by some maleficent spell into ravening wolves. The army of exiles, who preyed on the civilization in which they had been brought up, contributed as much as those who were Moors or Turks by birth to the rise of their adopted countries. There had always been piracy in the Mediterranean, but the Barbary corsairs would never have been able to achieve and maintain their three centuries of formidable power without the concourse of the renegades.

Their contribution was the more telling in that it was made at a time when Europe was rapidly outstripping Islam, once its superior in culture and sophistication, in skills and resources of every kind. Renegades and Christian slaves—the first voluntarily, the second under compulsion—were the chief agents for the transmission of technology, particularly in the military and naval fields, to the less advanced Islamic lands. 'The Turks have acquired through the renegades all the Christian superiorities', Philippe de Canaye observed in 1573.[39] It was the renegades who piloted the corsair ships in European coastal waters, divulged the weak spots in the Christian defences and the times and places where their countrymen would be most vulnerable. They plotted the capture of thousands of their fellows and the destruction of their homes. They 'build the galliots, cast the guns, manufacture the muskets and operate the war industries; they lay the ambushes and invent the different strategems which cause such harm to Christendom'.[40] An English mission sent to Morocco in 1727 to ransom captives found an Irish renegade in charge of the sultan's only cannon foundry,[41] and early in the following century the daughter of the English consul in Algiers noted that the only manufacturing industry of any note was a powder mill run by a Swede.[42]

The most important single innovation pioneered by the renegades was the introduction of the 'round-ship', or sailing ship of war, as an alternative to the traditional oar-propelled craft (Plate 3). This made it possible for the corsairs to extend their operations beyond the Straits of Gibraltar and led to the rise of Sallee as a new base for Atlantic piracy. Two notorious privateers are credited with leading roles in this development. One was the Dutchman, Simon Danzer, who appears never to have formally accepted Islam and, after many years of successful marauding, struck a secret bargain with the French. He was received back into grace, bringing with him a number of captured Jesuit priests and two much prized bronze cannons, the loss of which infuriated the Dey of Algiers and led to a crisis in France's relations with the Regency which was only ended with the restitution of the guns.

Another leading mentor of the corsairs was John Ward, a fisherman from the east coast of England who had served for a time with the Channel Squadron before launching out on a career of buccaneering. Ward sailed to Morocco where he fell in with Anthony Johnson, Bishop and other adventurous compatriots with whom he operated, first from Larache and then from Tunis. There he became intimate with Kara Osman, the Agha of the Janissaries who was the city's virtual ruler. In 1607 the Venetian ambassador to the Court of St James reported a rumour that Ward and his English followers, to the number of about 300, had offered to give up their career of piracy and return to England if they were granted the royal pardon. But no deal was struck. The Royal Proclamation of the following year, which declares that 'no English ship is to sell, bargain or exchange with them guns, powder, cordage and material of war, under pain of being held accomplices', specifically mentions Ward by name as a leading pirate. Later, he seems to have made similar overtures to the Grand Duke of Tuscany, promising to bring 150,000 crowns of his fortune with him if allowed to settle near Florence. Some said the corsair should be invited to Leghorn, from where he could operate against his former associates; others held that a man of his sort could never be trusted or his crimes forgiven. So Ward ended by abjuring his religion, taking the name of Yusuf Raïs, and dying of plague around the year 1622. An English sailor who knew him in his prime describes him as short and rather bald, with a swarthy beard and complexion— very bold, prodigal and profane, drunk from morning till night when in port, and totally ignorant of anything except sea-faring. The English ambassador to Venice calls him bluntly 'beyond doubt the greatest scoundrel that ever sailed from England''.[43]

By the eighteenth century the importance of the renegades in most of the Barbary states had declined. In Morocco they seem to have retained their influence somewhat longer, as we have noted from the status of the Irish gun-founder Carr, who

was in high favour with the sultan. The British Mission enter-
tained him to dinner and found him

> a very handsome man, very ingenious. . . . To us he seemed
> much to lament his condition and declared himself as much
> a Christian as ever. . . . He said that if he could get into
> Europe, he could easily put the Christians in a way to take
> this country; and though he was a Moor in religion, he
> boasted of the great service he had done the English in this
> country. . . . He drank with us very hard, and declared to us
> if it was not that he locked himself up every now and then,
> and took a hearty dose of wine, he could not have supported
> his spirits, when he came to think he was for ever lost to his
> country and friends. He stayed with us so late that his wife
> sent her brother to our house to bring him back; and before
> he left us he was so drunk that he fell down on his way home,
> and cut his nose and face very fiercely, and like to have
> broke his nose.

But once the Irishman had received the customary 'presents'
from the Mission, 'he came very seldom among us; and before
we left Mequinez [Meknes], we believed him as much a Moor
as any in the country, and as much in their interest'.[44]

A European who gained Muley Ismael's favour a few years
later was the duke of Ripperdá, surely one of the most remarkable turn-coats of all time. Starting life as a Dutch Protestant,
he embraced Catholicism and rose to become Spain's minister
of foreign affairs; ousted by his enemies, he then defected to
Morocco where he served for a time as the sultan's Grand
Vizier, commanded his armies, and spent his closing years
trying to persuade the Moors of Tetuan that he was the last of
the Prophets.[45] In Tripoli, too, renegades continued to wield
considerable influence. A Venetian traveller noted in 1765
that the Court there was composed mostly of renegades and
was dominated by its Maltese treasurer. But in Tunis, which
had a tradition of relative toleration of foreigners, renegades
now commanded little respect. 'For me', the Bey could observe
to an intending apostate, 'a pig still remains a pig, even if they
do cut off his tail.'[46]

In Algiers their stock fell still lower. This was partly due to the large number of deserters and would-be apostates from Oran—a riff-raff of scoundrels, convicts, and unfortunates, many of whom had been forced into debt to supplement their starvation rations and knew that acceptance by Islam would mean the remission of debts contracted whilst Christians. Morgan, resident in Algiers in the early eighteenth century, was struck by the change of attitude. 'Formerly', he wrote,

the Renegadoes of Barbary were a very considerable body in the state, the main bulk of their corsairs consisting of them, and were actually dreaded, even by the Turks themselves, lest they should side with the discontented natives and introduce the Christians. The Turks, then, could not well go to sea without them; whereas the case is now entirely otherwise. In former days, nay not very many years since, I have been credibly informed that nothing was more common to be seen in the streets of Algiers than parties of renegadoes, sitting publicly on mats, costly carpets and cushions, playing cards and dice, thrumming guitars, and singing *a la christianesca*, inebriating like swine, till the very last of the moon Shaaban [the Moslem fast of Ramadan], and in their drunken airs ridiculing, and even reviling, the Mahometans and their religion. At all which the Turks would commonly only shake their heads and smile; nay, the Pashas themselves, even such of them as were Turks, would only say 'Well, these renegadoes are neither Christians, Musulmans nor Jews; they have no faith, nor religion at all.' Whereas of later years, the case has been and still is very different. . . . Few are now in great esteem.[47]

8

Ransoms

A captive's first thought—unless he abjured or tried to escape—was to try to arrange his ransom. In the course of the seventeenth, eighteenth and early nineteenth centuries, as personal gain rather than religious fanaticism became the driving force, the ransom business grew into an ever more complex and sophisticated affair. It took many forms and involved many agents, in addition to the two specialized Religious Orders whose functions we shall be looking at more closely; merchan-go-betweens, individual philanthropists and charitable organit zations, municipalities and—increasingly—governments.

A small proportion of captives managed to raise and effect their own ransoms. These were the fortunate few possessing well remunerated skills—surgeons, for example—or men authorized to run taverns. D'Aranda mentions one tavern-keeper in Algiers who used his earnings to pay the ransoms of fellow-slaves; the king of Spain sent him a message commending his good work and promising a reward, but he ended his days in captivity.[1] Most slaves could only raise their ransoms through the help of their families. No obstacles were placed in the way of their communicating with friends and relatives at home, although their owners might try to discover the contents of their letters through informers. Communications were slow and difficult, and some letters never reached their destination. Those that did generally brought a generous response, though a family might be ruined by being forced to sell property or contract debts. Cervantes' sisters, for instance, sacrificed their modest dowries, but even when their mother had contributed what she could the sum proved insufficient and Cervantes generously renounced his share in it so that his captured brother could go free. Family solidarity might even go to the extent of one member voluntarily taking the place of another in captivity. In 1617, the son of the Sicilian Antonio de Vincenzo de Feltro was accepted as a hostage in Tunis so that his father could return home in order to raise the 400 escudos needed for his ransom.[2] But cupidity or callousness occasionally proved stronger than natural affections. In 1612 we find Pierre Sabatier, held a slave for two years in Tunis, issuing power of attorney to a maternal uncle in order to compel his father to take steps to arrange his ransom, and to use for that purpose the legacy left him by his deceased mother.[3] In 1640 the Trinitarian Lucien Hérault returned from Algiers with a similar authority from a married lady who had been captured together with her husband and brother, whilst her parents selfishly continued in the enjoyment of the captives' estates in France.

Sometimes a slave would be granted provisional liberty to allow him to return home to raise the ransom for himself and his fellows. Numerous cases of this kind are on record. In 1610, fourteen Knights of St John, then slaves of Othman Dey, were allowed to send one of their number back to Malta to raise their ransom and arrange an exchange with certain Tunisian captives held there.[4] Six years later, we hear of another group of captives at Tunis consisting of three priests, three Dominicans, and one layman, selecting one of their number, a friar, to arrange their ransoms in Sardinia; the following year the same group, apparently dissatisfied with the progress made, gave power of attorney to two other Sardinians to act for them and to require the friar to give an account of his labours on their behalf. The slaves thus released on parole generally seem to have proved worthy of the trust placed in them, for the practice continued to be widespread. Occasionally an individual captive was allowed to return home to arrange his ransom even without leaving a group of fellows as hostages; we have already noted the remarkable case of the Spanish fisherman, twice captured and twice sent back home to pay his ransom to the family of his renegade countryman (see p. 48).

It might be thought that the simplest way for a captive to retain his freedom would be by way of exchange. In practice, such transactions proved exceedingly difficult to arrange. In the first place, few exchanges were carried out on a one-for-one basis; the Moslems were generally able to insist on a ratio of two or three of their coreligionists for every Christian released. Speculators in slave-dealing were against them, for even where

ransoms were paid in addition to the exchanges, the profit
involved was likely to be small. Nor did the captains of either
Christian or Moslem galleys relish the prospect of losing
seasoned oarsmen. The French captains proved particularly
adept at circumventing or delaying royal orders for the release
of their Moslem galley-slaves. Sometimes the exchanges
proposed fell through on account of the illness, death, or
apostasy of the captives concerned.

The complications likely to arise in such cases can be well
illustrated from the account which Emanuel d'Aranda has left
of his adventures. He and his three Flemish companions were
captured in 1640 and eventually bought by Ali Piccinino. After
six months' captivity, hearing nothing from their families, they
petitioned their owner to allow one of them to go to Leghorn
to negotiate the ransoms for all four. Ali agreed, but demanded
a ransom of 2,000 patagons (or 1,500 if paid in Algiers) for
each; the Flemings protested that they were poor soldiers who
could not raise more than 500 a head. In the meanwhile, the
captives' families had located seven Moslems held prisoner in
Bruges, and two of their number were given provisional liberty
and returned to Algiers to negotiate an exchange. The rapacious
Ali was far from pleased; he had bought his slaves cheap in the
hope of fat ransoms, but the law required that Christians should
be exchanged against Turks for the price first paid for them.
He discovered however that Mustafa, one of the seven, was not
a Turk but a Morisco; so he agreed to let three Flemings go for
500 patagons each in exchange for the Turks, but demanded
1,400 patagons to complete the exchange of Mustafa and the
fourth. This sum was reluctantly paid by the Morisco's grand-
mother after fruitless attempts, by dint of threats and ill-
treatment, to induce the Christians to raise it. One of the
Flemings was released in order to escort the other Turks across
Europe from Bruges to Ceuta where the exchange was to be
effected. A last minute hitch threatened when it was reported
that one of the Turks had become a Christian whilst in
captivity and so should not be handed back. None of the
parties concerned, however, had an interest in pressing the
point; the Turk protested that he remained a good Moslem, the
exchange was completed, and d'Aranda and his comrades at
last found themselves free.

7   *left* A French slave in Algiers

right Pierre-Joseph Dumont, thirty-four years a slave in Barbary

9   Thanksgiving procession of ransomed slaves

Many random transactions were negotiated with the help of intermediaries—Jewish, Christian or even renegade merchants with business connections on both sides of the Mediterranean. Reputable merchants charged a fixed commission for their services. The powerful Lomellini family, for instance, who controlled the coral fisheries of Tabarca, an island ceded to the Genoese off the coast not far from the present Algerian-Tunisian border, handled most of the ransom business with Tunis, charging a modest 3% on each transaction, but giving their services free in the case of young Christian boys and girls. But many were less scrupulous. Mouette, who knew conditions in Morocco well, describes what too often happened. When a family in Europe learned that one of its members had been enslaved it would make over funds to a merchant house having a factor in Barbary. The money would generally be used to purchase goods which would be shipped out and sold. But the proceeds would not be made over to the intended recipient, who would be kept in ignorance of the affair. The family would be assured that the factor was doing everything possible to arrange matters, but that the affair must not be hurried or the slave-owner would raise his terms. Hearing no news from home and seeing no sign of any ransom, the captive would often grow desperate and apostatize.[5] Father Gracián, from his experience of Tunis, confirms that the intermediaries 'drag out the ransom or make it impossible, so that they can continue to make use of the money and double their gains, using all sort of devilish tricks to attain their aims'. He too cites cases of young captives driven to turn Moslem in their despair.[6]

The Christian merchants, in fact, found themselves in an ambiguous position. Some made fortunes by shipping stolen cargoes to Europe and re-selling them at enormous profit. However upright and compassionate they might be as individuals—and some were genuinely moved at the plight of the slaves and anxious to help them—it was to their advantage to keep the system of plunder and enslavement operating smoothly. They aroused the indignation of their captive countrymen who pestered them for money and food and blamed them for not doing more to secure their release. In 1791 the lives of the whole French resident community in Algiers, from the consul and Apostolic Vicar down, were threatened by desperate compatriots who had enlisted under the Spanish flag and then deserted, so that the French government was eventually blackmailed into agreeing to ransom them.[7] The instructions issued to French priests going to Barbary warned them 'not to show themselves too liberal towards the slaves they met with; not to answer for them or lend them money, however much they pressed for it, and whatever security they offered for it'.[8] Above all, no priest, merchant or sailor should do anything to help a slave escape; he, and probably the leaders of the whole community, would pay for such misplaced sympathy with imprisonment or death. Even the ex-slave Mouette recommends that merchants should steer a middle course between indifference and intimacy, and prudently confine their charity to helping the slaves when ill and providing food for them on church feast-days.[9]

The Jews, with their cosmopolitan connections, were specially active in the ransom business. Hated by the Christians, particularly by the Spaniards who had driven them from their country, they were often accused of tricking and exploiting the captives they were ostensibly helping. They seem in fact to have been no worse than other middlemen in this respect, and sometimes indeed more reliable. Father Gracián was amongst those who secured his release through their services. At first he had tried to arrange an exchange with two prominent Moslem corsairs held in Sicily, where the vicereine was sympathetic to the scheme. But it failed through the anti-Spanish malice of an Italian merchant, brother to the Bey's renegade major-domo, who persuaded his master that the priest was too valuable a prize to be surrendered in this way. Gracián then turned to the Jews of Tunis, one of whom—Simon Escanasi—had been arrested and his goods seized in Naples. Through his friends there Gracián secured the Jew's release and his return to Tunis with a loan of 600 escudos which he deposited with the Lomellini. The Bey, hard pressed at the time to find funds with which to pay his janissaries, agreed to a ransom of 1,900 escudos for Gracián, the balance to be advanced by the Lomellini against letters of credit on Naples. As soon as the priest had received his formal certificate of release, Escanasi, who had reason to suspect that the Bey would go back on the bargain once the janissaries had been paid, arranged for him to go into hiding until the French consul and the Lomellini could arrange his safe passage to Italy.[10]

Such vicissitudes and combinations were not uncommon before a captive could recover his freedom. Unlike France, which favoured the Trinitarians, and Spain, where the Mercedarians took the lead, Italy had a number of smaller organizations based on individual states and cities.[11] The oldest was the Real Casa Santa della Redentione de Cattivi, which operated from Naples with an initial endowment of 4,000 ducats annually. The Mercedarians had unsuccessfully tried to assert their control over the foundation, but a papal bull of 1581 precluded them from soliciting alms for ransom in the Kingdom of Naples. The Capuchin friars were chiefly responsible for the work of the Casa Santa until the mid-seventeenth century, when transactions were institutionalized through a system under which a slave could be 'imported' from Barbary and payment made at the agreed price to the owner's representative in Naples. Rome had its Arciconfraternita del Gonfalone, also operated largely by the Capuchins, who had the difficult task of redeeming captives who were subjects of the papal states without giving the impression of working on behalf of the Pope whom the Moslems assumed to be immeasurably rich! Bologna, Venice (working through the Trinitarians), Palermo (through the Lomellini) and other Italian cities had their own organizations. Some north European ports too, such as Hamburg and Lübeck, founded similar bodies in the seventeenth century and sent occasional missions to Barbary.

The Orders of the Most Holy Trinity and of Our Lady of Mercy were founded early in the thirteenth century, as we have already noted (pp. 12–15), for the common purpose of succouring and redeeming Christian captives. An element of not always pious emulation characterized their activities from the outset, particularly over the right to solicit alms. The Trinitarians complained that the Mercedarians were monopolizing the charity of the faithful and so making it impossible for them to raise money for ransoms; the Mercedarians countered with charges that the Trinitarians were discriminating against Spaniards in their redemptions. In the fifteenth century the Grand Master of the Trinitarians attempted to bring about a fusion of the Orders but was soon accusing his rivals of being not Mercedarians but mercenaries in the service of the king of Aragon, enemy of the French people whose alms they were misusing to ransom foreigners or 'dissipating in debauchery'.[12] The Emperor Charles V obliged the Orders to compose their differences and delimit their respective areas of operations. In later years they even carried out some joint redemptions, but the old rivalries were never far beneath the surface and prevented the best use being made of rare resources.

The first great upsurge of corsair activity under the Barbarossas found the two Orders in no condition to meet the new challenge. The Trinitarians were required under their Constitution to devote one third of their revenues to the work of ransom; but this was widely disregarded, and the upkeep of their houses and hospitals in Europe absorbed almost all their available funds. In the half century between the fall of Granada and the defeat of Charles V before Algiers the Mercedarians undertook some seventeen missions, some of them of minor importance, to Barbary. These were clearly insufficient to restore to liberty more than a tiny proportion of the men, women and children then being carried off into captivity. And since works of mercy are not the preserve of any one organization or body of men, however devoted, it is not surprising to find others outside the ranks of the official Redemptionist Orders answering the call to service. One such figure, though little remembered today, looms through the mist of pious legend in truly heroic proportions; that of Fernando de Contreras, a priest of Seville noted as a preacher, teacher of children and founder of orphanages, who undertook the first of his seven journeys to Barbary in 1532 at the age of sixty-one.[13]

Contreras first sought an audience of the dread Khair al-Din and requested his permission to ransom the captive children. It seemed a presumptuous and foolhardy request, for it was well known that the Moslems regarded it as highly meritorious to bring up young Christians in the faith of Islam. But though he was now master of Algiers, Barbarossa was faced with growing popular unrest and distress on account of a severe drought which not all the supplications of the marabouts had been able to end. Barbarossa agreed that the Christian children might go in procession to pray for rain, and if their prayers were answered, they could be ransomed. After three days of prayer and preparation, the procession set off carrying lighted tapers and intoning the litany—a scene never witnessed before in that Moslem city. Soon the tapers were extinguished by a down-pour which continued for three days. Barbarossa kept his word and Contreras returned to Spain with a shipload of children. The next year he was back again with more funds, but these proved quite insufficient for the vast number of captives who still remained. Having no possessions of his own other than his habit and his staff, Contreras proposed that he should leave the latter in pawn and send back money to redeem it once he had conducted his next batch of captives back to Spain. The Algerians were startled by this novel suggestion, but Bar-barossa, who had been impressed by the miracle of the rain and the priest's success in exorcizing an evil spirit from the corsair's brother-in-law, declared that he was a great marabout whose word was sacred. The staff was accepted as a pledge for 3,000 ducats and kept in the treasury until redeemed for that amount by French traders acting on behalf of a grateful Seville.

Contreras's third journey was to Tunis, where he was again well received by Barbarossa, but his work was cut short by news of Charles V's preparations to attack that city. There followed three journeys to Morocco and a final visit to Algiers. Twice more the priest left his staff in pawn, and twice again it was redeemed for 3,000 ducats by the city of Seville. The old priest, who declined the offer of a bishopric in order to continue his labours, was now venerated alike by Christians and Moslems, who attributed many miracles to him. A Moor, raising his arm to strike a slave with his scimitar, found it paralysed in mid-air through the saint's intercession; the *raïs* of a corsair ship with a captured Spanish merchantman in tow, meekly released his prisoners at his mere behest. The legal *testimonios de redenciones de cautivos*, particularly numerous around the year 1542, give more prosaic evidence of his work; we read of sixty-two men, women and children restored to freedom early in November, and 340 more later in the same month. No estimate is possible of the total ransomed by Fernando de Contreras, but few men can have laboured longer and more successfully on behalf of the victims of misfortune.

The Trinitarians and Mercedarians, however humble and

selfless as individuals, have advanced proud claims for their respective Orders. Even in Dan's day it was being said that the Trinitarians had already ransomed 30,720 captives and carried out 363 missions of redemption,[14] though a more sober historian of the Order has not been able to trace more than fifteen.[15] Later accounts speak of 900,000 Christians ransomed, and 9,000 redemptionists martyred in the process—totals which the same historian considers should be divided by ten to give the more realistic figures of 90,000 ransomed and 900 martyred.[16] For the Order of Mercy a painstaking but incomplete tally gives 68 missions and nearly 10,000 captives ransomed in the thirteenth century, over 13,000 in the fourteenth, between 8,000 and 8,500 in each of the two following centuries, over 10,000 in the seventeenth, and nearly 7,000 in the eighteenth. If some redemptions effected in South America and a few others made on an individual basis are included, this gives a total for the Order of Mercy of some 365 missions and over 57,000 captives ransomed.[17]

If the balance sheet, in terms of lives redeemed from slavery over the span of nearly five centuries, can be no more than the roughest of estimates, we may form a much clearer picture of the nature of the operations. Each mission of redemption required lengthy preparation. Its destination and composition had to be decided, permits obtained, and funds collected. The Redemptionists were the precursors of our modern fund-raisers. Part of their revenue came from legacies, the sale of property and valuables, church collecting-boxes, indulgences, fines (e.g. on clerics living with concubines) and 'alms-quests'. The latter were staged with great solemnity and ingenuity. Trumpeters, flautists and cymbal-players accompanied the friars who bore aloft a banner flying from a ship's mast. Heralds announced the forthcoming redemption and invited the people to give the names of kinsfolk in captivity and how much they could contribute towards their ransom. On the successful conclusion of the redemption, the ransomed captives themselves would appear in the procession to show that the money had been well spent and to incite the faithful to give even more generously. Sometimes theatrical representations or tableaux were staged to depict their miseries and their deliverance by the Redemptionists. Fraternities of lay tertiaries were formed to further the good work, specially in towns where the Order had no monastery, and special collectors known as *marguilliers* were authorized by letters patent to solicit alms for it. As early as 1228 the Trinitarians found it necessary to obtain a papal bull authorizing them to imprison swindlers posing as collectors.[18]

Once the General Chapter had decided to undertake a Redemption, the first step was to obtain a 'passport' or safe-conduct from the Moslem ruler concerned. This was obtained through the good offices of the Administrator of the Bagnio Hospital, the Apostolic Vicar, or some similar personage. The passport sometimes specified the value of the ransoms to be paid, the number of slaves to be ransomed from the ruler, and other particulars. Although such stipulations were often disregarded, it was better to have them rather than a document couched in purely general terms on which the ruler could then put his arbitrary gloss. The safe-conduct ensured that the ransom-ship would not be molested to and from its destination by the ruler's own subjects, but it offered no guarantee against corsairs who did not recognize his authority. Thus, in 1711, two ransom-ships returning to Cartagena after a successful mission to Algiers were intercepted by Tunisian corsairs and their occupants again reduced to slavery until the payment of an indemnity of 44,000 pesos to the sultan in Constantinople secured their release.[19]

The Redemptionists were also issued with documents from their own authorities, including permission to export the coins or bullion intended for the ransoms. At first they were forbidden to take merchandise, since friars should not dabble in trade, but this restriction was later lifted. Bales of cloth were found to be a particularly convenient form of currency; Chastelet des Boys tells us that he was ransomed in 1643 for 100 écus' worth of woollen cloth, coral and opium.[20] Every sort of currency circulated in the cities of the Barbary coast, but not all were equally welcome. In his day, Haedo tells us, the most prized were the Spanish silver coins known as reales, 'for they send them to Turkey and to Cairo, and from there onwards to the East Indies and as far as China and Tartary, bringing a profit to whoever takes them there. Nothing can be introduced into Barbary and Turkey which is more valued than Spanish reales.'[21] The gold escudo—so called from the escutcheon on its face—was worth about a dozen reales and began to replace the traditional ducat in the second half of the sixteenth century. Since the value of all currencies fluctuated, and the Redemptionists were constantly being assailed by complaints that their coins had been adulterated or tampered with, they sometimes preferred to bring in their funds in the form of bullion which could be turned into sequins in the Algiers mint. This was operated by Jewish craftsmen under close supervision.[22]

In addition to the ransom money, the Redemptionists had also to bring with them the 'presents' which immemorial custom decreed must be made to the ruler and his hierarchy of officials. The nature of these was sometimes specified in the 'passports'. In 1765 we find the emperor of Morocco insisting on cochineal —a commodity fetching astronomical prices at the time in Spain. The Redemptionists found it impossible to meet this demand and they prevailed upon him to accept instead a consignment of tea which he later pronounced to be no good. The number and cost of the presents had to be worked out and included in the Redemptionists' budget or they would other-wise incur crippling debts. Failure to make presents which their recipients regarded as appropriate to their rank and expectations caused great offence and jeopardized the prospects for the mission.

As soon as a ransom-ship reached a Barbary port, an official was sent to ascertain the value of the funds and goods on board. This formed the basis on which the numerous and heavy dues were calculated before the work of ransom could proceed. Dan states that in Algiers the Pasha (later, the Dey) was entitled to 10% of the total, and he lists sixteen other separate charges, either percentage or fixed rates, which had to be deducted. According to Laugier de Tassy, a century later, these dues amounted to nearly half of the Redemptionists' available funds and were computed according to the following scale:[23]

$$
\begin{array}{lll}
\text{The Dey: on merchandise} & - & 12\tfrac{1}{2}\% \\
\text{on cash} & - & 2\tfrac{1}{2}\% \\
\text{Customs} & - & 10\% \\
\end{array}
$$

Minister and chief scribes	—	4%
Port captain	—	7%
Guardian Pasha	—	17%
(on beylik slaves)		

A veritable battle of wits and wills had thus to be joined at the outset in order to salvage the greater part of the ransom money for its proper purpose. It is not surprising to learn that the Fathers felt justified in 'always trying to declare less than half of the real value of what they bring with them'.[24] Whilst the slaves unloaded the chests of money and bullion and carried them off to be checked, the Fathers were escorted to the Dey's palace and then lodged in a rented house known as the Casa de la Limosna.

The arrival of a ransom-ship moved the captives to a frenzy of excited hope (Plate 10). The Redemptionist Fathers customarily distributed a piastre a month (*la luna*) to those of their own nationality so that they could buy exemption from work and prepare their petitions, and they were given twenty-four hours' freedom from their fetters. The slaves also deposited with the Redemptionists whatever sums they themselves had been able to collect towards their ransoms. In their desperate anxiety to regain their freedom they tried every ruse. Forged letters were produced claiming that money was on its way to them or had already been entrusted to the Redemptionists' Order. Some said they would apostatize or take their own lives; others threatened those of the Fathers. Not a few concealed that they had contracted large debts which they would later expect the Fathers to pay off for them. The Redemptionists did their best to discover the truth but were ignorant of local conditions and often had to rely on untrustworthy intermediaries and interpreters. They also had to contend with the wiles of the owners who were no less anxious than their slaves to do a deal with the Redemptionists provided they could get what they demanded. Masters were chiefly concerned with getting rid of slaves who were too old or sick to be of much further use to them. Some even promised their slaves a commission if they could persuade the Fathers to pay up. Collusion between master and slave reached its most cynical pitch when young Christians, who had already decided to turn Moslem, waited until their ransom had been paid before abjuring. This was particularly apt to happen with Spanish deserters who feared punishment if they returned to Spain.

But before the private bargaining could begin, the Fathers had first to negotiate with the Dey for the purchase of an agreed number of slaves from his personal household. This customarily included his Chief Christian Secretary and others of the slave *élite*, for whom he demanded high prices, together with a number of lower grade kitchen servants, palace scavengers, gardeners and the like. The number of such privileged slaves, and the prices to be paid for them, were often specified in the 'passport', but the Dey generally ignored these undertakings and raised his terms, frequently also insisting on including some slaves of a different nationality. Such demands could doom negotiations from the outset. D'Aranda, whilst awaiting the conclusion of his own exchange at Tetuan, noted that the Spanish Trinitarians, who had come to do a deal with the Governor of that city, returned to Spain when he tried to force them to take thirty slaves from his household who were either Portuguese or French.[25] A despotic ruler held almost all the cards, but greed could sometimes lead him to overplay his hand. In 1737, for instance, the Dey of Algiers insisted on the exorbitant scale of 1,000 piastres for an ordinary slave, 5,000 for an officer, and 100,000 for each Knight of Malta. The Fathers refused to negotiate on that basis, and by the next year prices had fallen to 6–800 piastres for ordinary slaves and 22,000 and 10,000 respectively for the two knights.

A fall in the ransom price of slaves was exceptional and generally the temporary result of a particularly successful corsair raid or of some Christian defeat. The trend was otherwise markedly upward, partly in line with the general inflation of European prices and partly on account of the progressive decline in the number of slaves. The average ransom price of a Christian slave, reckoned in lire, rose from 400 in 1690 to 600 in 1710, jumped to 1,500 in 1729, reaching 1,800–2,000 around 1780, and 4,500 after 1790.[26] The 10,000 ducats paid in 1619 for the captured governor of Mazagan and the 16,000 demanded for the Portuguese Bishop Antonio de Govea the following year were then regarded as very high; but in 1798 the Sicilian prince of Paternó purchased his liberty for the gigantic sum of 300,000 escudos.

Once agreement had been reached and the ransom money paid over, each slave was handed a *teskere* or letter of emancipation. This gave the name of the slave and his master and the amount of ransom paid, and certified that the recipient was now a free man.[27] A personal description of the holder was sometimes added in the hope of discouraging the brisk trade in the sale or faking of *teskere*. The slaves were then mustered for a formal leave-taking before embarking on the ransom-ship. Elaborate precautions were taken to prevent other slaves slipping in amongst the ranks of the redeemed or sneaking on board as stowaways. The roll-call was read and the identity of the slaves checked several times over. Even so, a few ingenious slaves did manage to make their escape in this way. We read of one stowaway who escaped detection by standing for several hours up to his neck in a cask of drinking water at which his comrades came to quench their thirst without giving him away. The final hours before embarkation were a time of special anxiety for the Fathers, who might have to face a hostile send-off from the populace and knew how often a last-minute hitch could imperil the success of an entire mission. Once the final inspection of the ship had been completed, the sails, oars and rudder were restored, a bill of clean health was issued by the consul for the quarantine authorities at its intended destination, and the ship was free to sail.

The home-coming of the captives was not always the joyous experience they must have dreamed of. First, there was the long and tedious wait in quarantine. When this was over, the ex-slaves were expected to remain for a time at the disposal of the Redemptionist Fathers who vied with each other in staging the most moving and elaborate spectacles. Floats were sometimes constructed representing galleys manned with slaves toiling at the oars. Father Dan is credited with embellishing the processions with daintily dressed children representing angels, or as turbaned Turks leading along their captives on slender chains (Plate 9). Processions of ransomed captives were customary in southern Europe since at least the fourteenth century, and in France the last one is recorded as having taken place in 1785.[28] The route led, as far as possible, from monastery to monastery, taking in the chief towns from the place of disembarkation to the capital, where solemn services of thanksgiving would be held in the churches, the stations of the cross visited, and collections made to assist captives to meet the expenses of returning to their homes.

Some writers maintain that the spectacles were over-dramatized, and the participants made to march through the towns dragging chains the like of which they never had to wear in captivity. They were required to keep their hair and beards long, as was customary in the bagnios, and their appearance was so uncouth and frightening that some inhabitants of the smaller villages through which they passed would mistake them for brigands and barricade themselves in their houses. But most folk were moved with compassion and vied with each other in offering hospitality to the ex-slaves. The latter nevertheless frequently complained of the fatigue and discomfort of those enforced pilgrimages, which might last for several months, and objected to making public spectacles of themselves. The Chevalier Louis Castellane d'Esparron, for example, despite the fact that his huge ransom of 22,000 livres had been jointly raised by the Trinitarians and Mercedarians, refused their formal summons to participate. But many felt themselves bound to do so not only morally but legally, since the ransom contract contained a clause to that effect. Early enactments seem to have been very severe. In 1410, we find the governor of Majorca receiving twenty-eight prisoners who were pledged to remain at the disposal of their Mercedarian benefactors for a whole year. During that time, they were required to recite the prescribed prayers daily, to wear their prison garb, not to cut their hair without permission, and to refrain from gambling, swearing or frequenting brothels. They might not apply to the King, to the Pope, or to any of his representatives for exemption from these obligations, and disobedience was to be punished by fetters, imprisonment, and even torture.[29]

The earliest of the Trinitarian missions of which we have any detailed account is that undertaken by Fathers Juan Gil and Antón de la Bella in 1580, for Cervantes was amongst the 186 captives they ransomed. The friars found the Dey, his master, the grasping Hassan Veneziano, on the point of departing with his slaves and treasures for Constantinople. The modest sum which Cervantes' family had been able to raise fell far short of the 500 escudos demanded, but in a last minute effort to save him, they were able to collect the balance from donations made by his comrades. Cervantes' chains were struck off and he was put ashore just before the galleys left. Gil was a resourceful and tenacious negotiator who carried out three missions of redemption in Algiers. Haedo gives us a vivid picture of his activities, including his quarrel with a Turk, who had agreed to sell a young Spanish slave called Dorotea but later went back on his word on the pretext that he had been drunk. The Turk started beating the girl, Fray Juan tried to stop him, and the cry went up that he had raised his hand against a janissary and so should be sent to the stake or impaled. Another Moslem fortunately made the sensible suggestion that if the priest had struck the Turk, the latter should strike him back, and then they would be quits. There ensued a scene of tragicomedy which would have been much to the taste of the creator of *Don Quixote*; Haedo describes it as 'something to make one laugh as well as cry'. The bystanders joined in, punching and pinching the friar and finally leaving him bruised and half dead on the ground. Later, he took a Christian revenge on the Turk who was reprimanded and sentenced to the bastinado, by spreading his mantle over him and obtaining a stay of execution. But poor Dorotea remained in slavery.[30]

Other Trinitarian Redemptions ended more tragically. In 1609 three Spanish Fathers, Monroy, Aguila and Palacios, were on the point of leaving Algiers after ransoming a number of slaves, when a report was received that a Genoese galley had captured a shipload of Moslems. An exchange was arranged, but a ten-year-old girl called Fatima remained missing. The child's family was influential and succeeded in getting the Trinitarians and the slaves they had ransomed retained in reprisal. Fathers Aguila and Palacios perished soon afterwards in their dungeon, whilst the survivor, Father Monroy, was later released but forbidden to return to Spain. He devoted the rest of his life to selfless work amongst the slaves. Fatima appears to have been taken to Sicily where she became a nun.[31]

Another Trinitarian who died in captivity was Father Lucien Hérault, victim of the dissensions between the Mercedarian and Trinitarian Orders as much as of the malice of the Moslems. After completing a successful redemption in 1643, Father Hérault returned two years later on a further mission to Algiers. There a Mercedarian, Father Brugière, had been left pending the settlement of a debt of 12,000 escudos contracted by his Order. Father Hérault was commanded to repay this out of the ransom money he had brought with him. This the Trinitarian refused to do, explaining that the funds belonged to different Orders and were intended for different purposes. The Moslems, who never bothered their heads about such niceties, thereupon threw him into prison and resold the captives he had ransomed in order to repay Father Brugière's creditors. In prison, Father Hérault quickly sickened and died. His death was much lamented by the slaves who looked upon him as a matryr. Even the Moslems shared in their veneration to the extent of permitting their captives three days of rest for the priest's obsequies.[32]

The fullest accounts of the Mercedarians' activities probably come from the pen of Father García Navarro, who led two missions of redemption to Algiers and one to Tunis between 1722–5.[33] They throw interesting light on conditions prevailing when the corsairs' trade had begun to decline but the lot of the slaves and the difficulties faced by the Redemptionists remained as onerous as ever. The first mission was organized jointly by the Mercedarian Provinces of Castile, which had contributed more than half the funds (including 16,000 pesos raised by the Franciscans), and Andalusia, each being represented by two Redemptionists. The Order's American Provinces also sent contributions. Besides the Fathers, the mission included an apothecary and a surgeon for the bagnio hospital, and thirty Moors who were returning home after obtaining their freedom. Before the mission left Cartagena there occurred one of those incidents which the Algerians were adept at exploiting as pretexts for complicating the work of redemption and increasing their demands. A Moslem woman who wanted to return to Africa made a scene because she was not allowed to take with her a three-year-old daughter who had been baptized without the mother's consent during an illness of which she had seemed likely to die. The child had recovered, but the Church would not allow such a tender member of its flock to run the risk of apostasy by being brought up amongst Moslems.

After they had reached Algiers and watched the treasure-chests being carried up the steep streets by slaves 'who leapt and ran for joy, for captivity was far heavier for them to bear', the Fathers were summoned to their first audience. They found the Dey, accompanied by his four chief ministers, squatting on a cushion in his palace courtyard. Whilst the gold and silver was being counted and 3% (more than the proportion stipulated in the 'passport') set aside for him, one of the scribes read out letters sent by Moslems living in Cartagena alleging that they were being maltreated. A Moor who had returned with the mission commented that this was not true, and that some of the Moslems were doing very well for themselves there. He was supported by one of the ministers, a venerable old man who observed that he knew of no such ill-treatment; the letters had probably been written as an excuse for not returning. The Fathers may be said to have won this opening round, but it was to prove their only success.

The Redemptionists were then conducted to their lodgings in the Casa de la Limosna where they had to confer with their interpreter about the 'presents' they should bestow. This man, they were mortified to discover, was a renegade Frenchman, and an ex-Huguenot to boot, so that 'the Devil had gained little or nothing from his apostasy'. It was decided to give the Dey a ring worth 113 pesos (which he affected to despise), two sets of clothing, tobacco, chocolate, some boxes of *turón* and barrels of Seville olives. A distribution of caftans, of various colours and qualities, was also made according to the rank of each recipient. The presentation of gifts was followed by a round of visits to leading Europeans—the Apostolic Vicar, a venerable Trinitarian in charge of the chapels, the French consul, 'a man of pacific nature, well disposed towards the Spaniards, to the extent of sometimes helping them to escape, at great personal risk, and smuggling them aboard French ships', and even the English consul, since 'we need everyone'. Only then, and in the intervals of dealing with a swarm of visitors, particularly Jewish intermediaries, were they able to visit the slaves in their bagnios.

When the Mercedarians were summoned to start negotiations

for the redemption of the Dey's slaves they were kept waiting in the courtyard where the groans of a slave who was being bastinadoed for a trifling theft were no doubt intended to impress them with the ruler's despotic power. They were then conducted up a narrow flight of steps to a small audience-chamber hung with pistols and scimitars which were kept there less for ornament than for defence against mutineers. They found the Dey unimpressed by their presents and angrily brandishing a letter of complaint from the Moslem woman whose child had been detained in Cartagena. The 'passport' issued to the Mercedarians specified that they should ransom four of his personal slaves, all Spaniards. The Dey insisted on their taking twelve, including three Dutch Protestants, at 1,000 pesos a head. Disclaiming anything which the 'passport' might have said with *Mi no escribir*—which was true enough, for he had been an illiterate camel-driver before starting his career in the Ottoman service—the Dey declared that all Christians were equally the children of their God, and as for some not being Spaniards, he would send a letter to the king 'as long as this'—here he held out his arm—to explain matters. Father García replied that the heretics were already lost souls and could not be taken in preference to Catholics, even were the king to order it. The Dey cut short his arguments with the scandalous words *Lo que mi querer, querer el Señor Dios; i así lo querrá el rey de España*—'What I want, the Lord God wants—and the King of Spain had better want it too.' He then gave the Fathers an ultimatum; they would buy his twelve slaves at the price stated or leave Algiers within four hours. The Spaniards withdrew in great indignation; but they had to accept the Dey's terms, as well as agree to take a further twenty-three of his lesser slaves at 500 pesos a head.

The extortions of the Dey and of other high officials who similarly forced the Mercedarians to take their personal slaves at high prices sadly depleted the funds available for those in the bagnios and private ownership. Men jostled and fought each other in their eagerness to get their names onto the ransom list; one who had had his included and then deleted fell to the ground in a fit. The Redemptionists tried to give preference 'to those most in danger of losing their faith, and those whom we were most under an obligation to buy on account of donations

10 Arrival of Redemptionist Fathers on a ransom mission

11 An ambassador negotiating the release of captives

12 English slaves escaping in a home-made boat

and commissions received on their behalf', whilst the Dey tried to palm off on them the old and sick. To ransom some of the more distinguished captives was quite beyond their means; for Don Baltasar de Villalba, for instance, taken fifteen years before at Oran and now in his eighty-fourth year, 30,000 pesos was still demanded, and he was left to die in captivity. What specially mortified the good Fathers was to see their ransom money wasted on young rascals who, after being freed, abjured in collusion with their former masters. Potential defectors were accordingly kept under lock and key in the Casa de la Limosna until they embarked on the ransom-ship, but even so half a dozen such apostasies occurred.

Four hundred and twenty-five captives were redeemed in Father García's first mission to Algiers, and another 283 in the second. His account ends with complaints about the ex-slaves' ingratitude and insolence towards their benefactors, their tiresome demands for the best food, comfortable beds, and coaches in which to travel. He berates the Franciscans for claiming credit for the redemption, though they had contributed only a trifling sum towards its cost, and proudly refuses a present they wished to give him as a peace offering. He pours scorn on the Reformed or Discalced branch of his own Order for claiming that 'these self-styled saints (*sánticos*) should act as ransomers with the funds raised by the Calced', and as a proud Castilian he reproves his Andalusian brethren for being too ready to offer large sums to free their fellow countrymen. Decidedly, for all his energy and dedication, the distinguished Mercedarian cannot have been an easy man to work with.

Father García's third mission was to Tunis where a relatively high proportion of the 370 captives ransomed were women. His account affords interesting insights into their varied destinies. One 22-year-old Spanish woman, with a husband in Spain, had been kept in the seraglio where she had managed to remain a Christian and resist the Bey's advances; his jealous, middle-aged wife, a Genoese renegade, anxious to get rid of a potential rival, persuaded the Bey to sell her. But another young woman, a Greek, in whom the Bey showed little interest, had become a favourite of his wife, who wanted to keep her. She too had remained a Christian, thanks largely to the promise of a fellow captive that he would marry her once they both regained their freedom. This must have been a rare case of a slave romance with a happy ending; the man was ransomed first, and the woman found him waiting for her when she too at length regained her liberty. Two Valencian women, a mother and her thirteen-year-old daughter, were owned by a rich Moor. His son wished to marry the girl and did his best to prevent her being ransomed. But the father, attracted by the high prices offered for them, overruled his son and sold them both. Another thirteen-year-old girl, whose mother had died in captivity, was being kept as a bride for her owner's son. She seemed quite contented with her lot and refused the offer of a ransom. Two Christian slave-girls were owned by the same master, who had accepted a ransom for them; at the last moment, one of them, seduced by gifts of jewels and other blandishments, stayed behind and apostatized; her master kept the ransom money for her dowry.

The Redemptionists were not only concerned with the ransoming of slaves; they also did what they could to relieve the sufferings, and to strengthen the faith, of the many who remained. To the same end many other priests, some captives themselves, others who had answered the call to labour in Barbary, devoted often heroic efforts. Some fell victim to outbursts of religious fanaticism or a coldly calculated reprisal. Legend tells of the twelve friars sent by St Francis to Morocco and martyred there for preaching the gospel, and of Ramón Lull, the Majorcan mystic and philosopher, stoned to death for the same offence. Many more recent examples, such as those of the harmless old Carmelite friar Father Garão, and Father Aranda, carried off in broad daylight by Algerian raiders near Valencia, figure in Father Haedo's Martyrology. The list could be continued until well into the seventeenth century with the case of Gian Battista da Ponto, lynched in Tripoli in 1653 for trying to reconvert the Bey, a renegade from Chios, and a few years later, of Pedro de la Concepción, sent to the stake after he had rushed into a mosque, crucifix in hand, denouncing the errors of Mohammed.

The records tell too of many lives of less sensational sacrifice; the Capuchin staying on in captivity and using his ransom money to buy a plot of land where Christians could be decently buried instead of just thrown into the sea; a bishop of Limerick —he is simply referred to as Tomás Hibérnico—captured on his way back to Ireland from Rome in 1591, who spent his ransom on a permit allowing him to travel round Barbary ministering to the needs of the slaves; Father Angeli, as divine in his charity as his name, tending the sick, composing quarrels, and telling the rapacious Ali Piccinino to his face that he would go straight to hell; Father Monroy tending his flock of captives for thirteen years whilst the Moslems vainly sought the return of the converted Fatima; Father Gracián, preaching from his barrel-pulpit, exhorting, advising, consoling, contriving ransoms for his fellow slaves, and withal so loaded with chains himself that even the Moslems murmured at the inhumanity of their Pasha.

Two institutions—if that is not too grand a word—gradually evolved to brighten the catacomb-like existence of the Christian slaves; the bagnio hospitals and chapels. The earliest hospital seems to have been started in Algiers in the middle of the sixteenth century, but it must soon have fallen into decay since we find Friar Bernardo de Monroy and his companions re-founding it around 1612, and the fanatical Pedro de la Concepción zealously enlarging it before his martyrdom. The Father Administrator, always a Trinitarian of the Castilian province of that Order, became an important personage. He was allowed to import food, clothing and medicine (some of which was resold to Moslem patients) free of duty, also wine which the Christian tavern-keepers bought from him at high prices.[34] In addition, each ship putting into Algiers from a Catholic country was required to pay hospital dues, and a small levy for the same purpose was made on crew members and passengers. In their heyday, each of the five bagnios in Algiers had a small hospital attached to it, but by the end of the eighteenth century the number had sunk to one. Father Comelin, who took part in a Redemption in 1720, found them run in very orderly fashion. Morning and evening prayers were punctually performed.[35] No woman was allowed in, but the apothecary might be sent to attend a female patient in her home. Masters had first to give their permission before a slave could be accepted for hospital treatment, and had also to deposit a third of a dollar for his funeral expenses, recoverable if he got better. Slave-owners thus got their personal property looked after cheaply, but a brutal Guardian Pasha sometimes refused to excuse his sick slaves from work and insisted on their being discharged from hospital. In Morocco, where conditions were in general so much worse, an eighteenth century traveller paints an un-expectedly favourable picture of the monastery hospital established by the Franciscans at Meknes—'delightfully situated for prospect', run by five friars, a lay brother and a surgeon, with accommodation for a hundred though there were few patients there at the time, and enjoying the protection of the sultan 'upon account of the yearly presents they make him, and because they take care of his sick slaves'.[36]

In the early seventeenth century, according to Father Dan's account, Algiers had three bagnio chapels, served by seven priests, who celebrated mass and preached every Sunday. Friar Bernardo de Monroy has left us a remarkable report, written in the fourth year of his captivity, describing the religious life centring round the bagnio chapels. Easter and other feasts of the Church were celebrated with devotion, and friendly Moslems would even lend ornaments for the occasion. Once, in a time of great drought, the Christians were allowed to go in procession through the streets, and—as in the days of Father Contreras—the heavens were opened in answer to their prayers.[37] Protestants—mainly English, Dutch and Huguenots—were of course regarded by their Catholic fellow prisoners as heretics and had no recognized facilities for worship. But we read of a captured Church of England clergyman holding informal services in a private house which were attended by seventy or eighty persons (see p. 139).

Tunis, where Father Gracián used to say mass on an impro-vised altar before dawn for his 600 fellow-captives, later had several chapels, and allowed the Christians more freedom of worship than anywhere else in Barbary. The French traveller Jean Coppin, who visited the city in 1640, found as many candles burning in one of the chapels 'as in the greatest church of Christendom'. His satisfaction was however somewhat marred by the sight of a corsair who entered and casually lit his pipe at one of the candles.[38] When Father García Navarro visited Tunis in 1736 he was told that the lamp burning before a statue of Santa Lucía was kept supplied with oil by pious Moslems, who believed that the intervention of that saint had saved a previous Bey from being blinded by a wicked uncle.[39]

Tripoli, too, had two bagnio chapels, dedicated respectively to St Michael and St Anthony, though there was often a shortage of priests to serve them. Each year the prisoners elected two representatives who were responsible for making monthly collections to cover expenses.[40] Captives of the Greek Orthodox faith had their own chapel, dedicated to St George, and likewise supported their own priests, towards whom the Catholic Redemptionists seem to have had a patronizing attitude. When the Trinitarians visited the city in 1700 they talked to one of these priests and were gratified to discover that his views on Catholic teaching and rites did not appear too erroneous. They even thought of trying to include him in their Redemption until they discovered that he was a married man with eight children and that he steadfastly rejected any idea of relegating his wife to a convent.[41]

In Morocco, according to Dan, the slaves had no chapels, but in one *mazmorra* they had put together two tables to form an altar and decked it with paper ornaments, before which they would chant litanies to the Virgin and perform other devotions night and morning.[42] D'Aranda paints a similar picture of fervent devotion in Tetuan where, he tells us, the captives raised such a noise scourging themselves at night during Lent that passers-by thought they were trying to break out and called out the guard.[43] The Dominican who led their devotions seems to have been a man of sense and authority who prevented them raising the large sum of four gold sequins for which a Moor was trying to sell them an image of the Virgin, and beat the man down until they got it for a trifle.

Provided the Christians were not too provocative in the exercise of their religion, the attitude of the Moslems was normally one of tolerance. Outbursts of fanaticism did occur, specially at times of crisis or when reports came in of Moslems suffering at the hands of Christians. During a drought in the days of Hassan Veneziano, the marabouts urged that the slaves should be forbidden to celebrate mass, and a number of sacred images which had been taken from Christian galleys and displayed hanging upside down on the ramparts were hacked to pieces and burned.[44] During a still more severe drought some years later, the Christians were again blamed, and there was talk of destroying even their hospitals as well as their chapels;[45] instead, apparently through the intervention of the French consul, they were allowed to go out in procession and the rains miraculously came (see p. 124). In 1634 rumours reached Algiers that Moslem captives in Malta were being hindered in the observance of their religious rites. In retaliation, bands of armed Moslems broke into the chapels during mass, overturning the chalices and seizing other sacred vessels and ornaments, which were either burned or later sold back.[46] Again, in 1762, following reports that Moslem slaves were being ill-treated in Cartagena, the Trinitarians serving the hospital were fettered and sent out to work; the chapels were closed but reopened two weeks later.[47] The use of images and pictures must have given constant offence to Moslem zealots. Father García refers to a fine picture of St Peter Nolasco, founder of his Order, which was hanging in a chapel in Algiers in replacement of a similar picture destroyed by the Moslems. Some paintings may have been tolerated on account of the anti-Jewish feelings shared by Christians and Moslems alike. We read of one showing Christ being scourged by the Jews, and even of a dummy, dressed as a Jew, hanging from a tree in the bagnio courtyard with a purse in his hand. Many Moslems came to see it, sometimes forcing Jews to come along too.[48]

In the second quarter of the seventeenth century the Church took an important step towards providing more continuous care for her captive flock. St Vincent de Paul, the enigma of whose personal experience of slavery we have already noted, founded his 'Congregation of the Missions', which established permanent posts in Algiers and Tunis under an Apostolic Vicar vested with general responsibility for the spiritual—and as far as possible the material—welfare of the Christian slaves. These Lazarist priests, as they came to be called, were also chaplains to the French consulates in those cities, and on occasion found themselves serving, often for considerable periods, as acting consuls. This proved an unfortunate development, since France was embarking on a period of strained

relations with the Regencies and the priest-consuls found themselves drawn into the imbroglio. Soon they were at loggerheads
with the powerful mercantile interests of the city of Marseilles
on the question of supplying forbidden war material to the
Barbary corsairs. The French Government, and even the
Papacy, had shown little interest in enforcing the ban, but the
Lazarists insisted on its observance. The merchants complained that they were being ruined, whilst the Moslems
denounced the priests' stand as a hostile act.

The slaves proved another source of embarrassment to the
Lazarist consuls. The latter might be men of admirable
charity, compassion and meekness; but, as a leading French
historian has tartly observed, 'Christian humility and the
craving for martyrdom are not consular virtues; the man who
represents France in a foreign land must represent her with
pride, and not forget that if he is struck, the whole nation is
insulted'.[49] The term of office of Barreau (then a Lazarist
lay-brother, later a priest) proved particularly disastrous. His
trouble seems to have been that he was 'incorrigibly good'. The
consul could never resist a plea for help, even from the shiftiest
of suppliants; he offered himself as surety for slaves unable or
unwilling to raise their own ransom and for merchants on the
brink of bankruptcy, and quickly overspent the funds available
to his congregation and to the consulate. St Vincent warned
that his indiscriminate charity could only harm his mission, the
consulate, and ultimately the captives themselves. Barreau
was repeatedly imprisoned and maltreated by the Dey of
Algiers eager to make the most of the unexpected opportunity
of humiliating and blackmailing a nation which, weakened by
its internal troubles, had ceased to prove a valued ally and
commercial partner.

In 1673 the Apostolic Vicar, Father Le Vacher, reluctantly
assumed charge of the consulate, whose official incumbent had
left following a row over the escape of some slave stowaways.
The Lazarist Father was a prudent man with a long experience
of the Barbary states. At first he was able to secure some
concessions, including the release of a number of Frenchmen
seized whilst on a pilgrimage. But fresh trouble soon followed;
there were more complaints about stowaways, and the Moslem
galley-slaves whose release the French Government had

promised in exchange for the pilgrims were not produced. Le Vacher was imprisoned, and in October 1681 Algiers declared war on France. Within one month, the corsairs had taken twenty-nine French ships and hundreds of prisoners. The following year Algiers concluded a treaty with France's enemy, England. Admiral Duquesne was ordered to sail to the corsair city and destroy it 'from top to bottom'. The admiral, rejecting an attempt by Le Vacher to mediate, bombarded Algiers, which defended itself vigorously, and then withdrew.

In June 1683 the French warships were back, and again the admiral spurned Le Vacher's proffered mediation, contemptuously declaring that he was more Turk than Christian. The Dey, under the threat of the warships' guns, began reluctantly to collect and hand over the Frenchmen held captive in the city. By the beginning of July, it was claimed that there were no more French slaves in Algiers. A group of leading Moslems, including the redoubtable renegade Mezzomorto— so dubbed after he had been found lying half dead on the battle-field—were held by the French as hostages whilst the Dey tried to raise the heavy indemnity demanded by Duquesne before the French would lift the blockade. Mezzomorto persuaded the French admiral that his influence was so great in Algiers that, if he was released, he could collect the money. So Mezzomorto was put ashore, where he promptly murdered the Dey, took command, and resumed vigorous hostilities. He sent an arrogant message to Duquesne threatening that if the French renewed their bombardment, he would fire off from the cannon's mouth all the Christians he could lay hands on. It was no empty threat. A mob sacked the French consulate, seized Le Vacher and carried him to the mouth of a cannon where, with twenty other French residents, he met his end.

Three years later Father Montmasson, Le Vacher's successor as Apostolic Vicar, was among a fresh batch of victims when another French admiral, Marshal d'Estrées, tried once more to bombard Algiers into surrender. His murder was even more brutal, for he was castrated and half-lynched by a bloodthirsty mob whilst being dragged to the cannon. D'Estrées sailed back home after reducing much of the city to ruins. Though they did not succeed in reducing the Barbary states to complete submission by such methods, the French had convinced them by the end of the seventeenth century that, in future, they would be wise to live and trade in peace with France. On the rest of the world they could continue to make war as they wished.

9

The English Slaves

English merchant ships had begun to venture into the Mediterranean in the first decades of the sixteenth century. It was not,
however, until the 1580s, whilst Philip II was preparing the
'Enterprise of England', that they appeared there in any great
number. They came in search of new outlets for their cloth,
salted fish, tin, iron and gunpowder, and found ready buyers
not only in European ports, but amongst the subjects of the
Sublime Porte. In 1581 the Levant Company was formed and
rapidly prospered. The following year saw the arrival in
Constantinople of William Harborne, Queen Elizabeth's new
envoy, and the granting of Capitulations specifying the trading
rights of English merchants.

Some of the new trade found its way to the Regencies. But
piracy was by now too lucrative and firmly entrenched a
business to be renounced, even in consideration of a nation
increasingly hostile to the corsairs' traditional enemy, Spain.
The first Englishmen to be enslaved had probably been
volunteers in foreign service, but the number of English
sailors taken from their own ships soon grew large enough to
cause the bishop of London, in 1567, to request Cecil to allow
collections to be made for their ransom.[1] There were Scots too
among the captives, including the Master of Morton and the
Master of Oliphant, on whose behalf Robert Oliphant petitioned the queen in 1582 for permission to fit out an expedition.
The project must have come to nothing, for seven years later
enquiries were still being made as to their fate. In 1583 the
queen granted a safe-conduct to Edmund Auncell, Richard
Thomson and others to sail the *Unity* to Algiers to redeem
their countrymen. Of the misadventures which had landed
these unfortunates in captivity we know almost nothing. One
early victim was the *Swallow* of London, amongst whose crew
was a youth called Fowlie, son of a Bristol merchant, who

turned Turk, took the name of Hassan, and rose to become treasurer in the Dey of Algiers' household. In 1586 we find 'Hassan Agha' corresponding with Harborne, who commends his 'Christian mind and English heart', pledging his services to help secure the release of his countrymen, and apparently hoping thereby to regain the favour of the queen.[2]

To obtain Capitulations promising fair treatment for English traders was one thing, and to see them respected by the corsairs quite another. Queen Elizabeth was soon writing to the sultan to complain that 'some of our subjects of late, at Tripoli in Barbary, and at Argier, were by the inhabitants of those places (being perhaps ignorant of your pleasure) evill intreated and grievously vexed'.[3] Ambassador Harborne had already made a similar and fruitless *démarche* direct to the Dey through a leading English merchant in Algiers. His correspondent— probably John Tipton, the Levant Company's factor, whom he was to appoint consul two years later—replied that neither the Dey nor his captains would undertake not to interfere with English shipping, but boasted rather that they would find some pretext to break the peace and, if need be, tear up the sultan's safe-conducts.[4] The Dey, Hassan Pasha, did himself on occasion issue a safe-conduct to an English merchant, but a letter addressed to him—as 'King of Algiers'—in July 1584 by Sir Edward Osborne, Lord Mayor of London and director of the Levant Company, complained that the Capitulations were still being disregarded and English ships unlawfully seized.[5] One such case is specifically mentioned. The *Mary Martin*, returning to England two years before with a cargo from Patras, had been attacked by two Algerian galleys, most of the crew slain or drowned, and the rest were still being held as slaves. The letter ended with an appeal that they should 'be set at libertie and returned into their country'.

One member of the captured crew survived to record his misadventures, and very strange, harrowing and protracted these proved to be.[6] Matters were undoubtedly made worse for Richard Hasleton by the fanaticism of his Protestant convictions. Concealing the fact that he was an experienced gunner, he toiled for five years in an Algerian galley until the latter was wrecked off Formentera, where the survivors gave themselves up. Denounced by his fellows as a Lutheran heretic,

Hasleton was sent to Palma where he was imprisoned and interrogated. His ordeals left his fierce Puritan spirit un- crushed. When given a crucifix to kiss, he boasts that 'I did spit in the Inquisitor's face'. He was consequently confined to a dungeon from which he escaped, was recaptured, and sub- mitted to various forms of torture in an attempt to make him recant. 'Where I thought to find such favour as one Christian with another', he bitterly recalls, 'I found them now more cruel than the Turks.' After a time, Hasleton escaped again, found a small boat and a hatchet with which he cut a branch from an olive tree, and fixing his cloak on it to serve as a sail, he entrusted himself to the sea. He was eventually cast back on the Barbary coast near Djidjelli, where he was given his first square meal in six years by an old peasant, 'rather a Christian than a Turk'. Refusing offers of money, land and a wife, if only he would apostatize, he made his way back to Algiers where he was recognized by his former master, bastinadoed, and put again in the galleys. He was eventually ransomed by 'an honest merchant of London', and returned to England, after more than ten years spent in various forms of captivity.

Two years after the sinking of the *Mary Martin* another incident occurred which threatened a further disruption of the English trade. The *Jesus*, a 100-ton ship chartered by the Levant Company, reached Tripoli and took on a cargo of sweet oils. All seemed to be going smoothly until a Frenchman called Sonning, who was travelling with her as a supercargo and trading on his own account, tried to smuggle aboard a European who was being held as surety for debt. Sonning persuaded the master of the *Jesus* to weigh anchor with the stowaway, but his game was discovered by the Turks, who prevented the ship from sailing, swarmed aboard and rifled everything within sight. Sonning and the master were hanged from the city ramparts and the rest of the crew enslaved and sent to the bagnio, where many of them died of the plague. The eleven survivors were only freed after Harborne had sent an embassy representative, accompanied by an official of the sultan, to Tripoli to settle matters.[7]

The affair had a dramatic and bloody sequel. Soon after the release of the *Jesus* survivors, a Maltese renegade stole a brigantine and made off, taking a dozen Christian captives with him. In an explosion of fury, the Turkish soldiery turned on Ramadan Pasha, the Bey of Tripoli, and killed him. The murdered man's family was packed off to Constantinople, together with his Christian slaves. These included four young Englishmen: a cabin-boy who had jumped his ship at Djerba and turned Turk, John Nelson, a renegade and son of a yeoman of the Queen's Guard, and two members of the crew of the *Jesus*, Smith and Burgess, to whom Ramadan's son had taken a fancy and forcibly circumcised. These four attempted to stage a mutiny and take over the galley. Nelson and the cabin-boy were slain in the fighting, and Smith and Burgess put in chains to be hanged in Constantinople. But off Cephalonia the galley was intercepted by a stronger Venetian force. All the Moslems on board, including Ramadan Pasha's family, were put to the sword; Smith and Burgess, since they were found to be circumcised, would have shared the same fate had not the Christian slaves testified to their forced conversion and attempted mutiny. In an effort to placate the Porte for the killing, the Venetians later had their commander executed and the prize returned. But the 150 Christians on board the galley, including the two young men from the *Jesus*, regained their liberty.[8]

Despite such incidents, relations with the Barbary states began to improve. Since 1585, England was officially represented in Algiers by a consul—Tipton, of the Levant Company. As preparations proceeded in Spain's Atlantic ports for the dispatch of the great Armada, English ships were able to call at North African ports not only to trade, but to refit or to sell a captured Spanish prize. In 1586, five English merchantmen trading with the Levant were waylaid by Spanish galleys attempting to intercept them on their return. After a running fight, they put into Algiers where they were well received. The Pasha, an Albanian renegade, issued a proclamation that no one, on pain of death, should injure or molest the English. His orders were obeyed by all but the enslaved Spanish captives 'who took all opportunities of showing their malice, by words and gestures; and one of them, meeting an English sailor straggling in a by-place, stabbed him in the side with a knife, though not mortally'.[9] The Pasha was informed, 'and sending for the English officers, caused him [the Spaniard] to be drubbed to death in their presence'. The treatment of English visitors varied according to the mood of the Moslem ruler and the circumstances of the moment. An Englishman calling at Algiers early the following year found fifteen of his countrymen still detained as slaves, whilst another traveller to Tunis, in the same year, noted the plight of thirteen Englishmen there, 'very ill used by the Moors, who forced them to leave their barke'.[10]

Matters continued much in this vein until the end of Elizabeth's reign. Hostility to Spain brought Moslems and Protestants together, though the latter, being looked upon as still Christians of a sort, were sometimes treated by the corsairs as their natural prey. On 6 April 1602, the queen addressed a letter to the Dey of Algiers rehearsing the complaints she had received of the injuries and injustice done to her subjects, and threatening to appeal to the sultan if redress was refused.[11] She reproached the Dey for showing too much favour to their mutual enemies the Spaniards, whom the queen declared were better treated than her own subjects. But the old queen was nearing the end of her reign and the pro-Spanish party was gaining the ear of her successor. The days of the alliance, such as it was, between England and the Barbary states were numbered, and the bagnios were soon to open their doors to ever larger contingents of English slaves.

In 1603 Queen Elizabeth died and England made peace with Spain the following year. Privateering had proved a profitable occupation during the years of declared or undeclared war, and many out-of-work adventurers threw in their lot with the corsairs. 'The great profit that the English bring to the country', the French Ambassador de Brèves wrote in 1606,

> their profuse liberality and the excessive debauches in which they spend their money . . . have made them cherished by the janissaries above all other nations. They carry their swords at their side, they run drunk through the town . . . they sleep with the wives of the Moors . . . in brief every kind of debauchery and unchecked licence is permitted them.[12]

The activities of these renegade Englishmen, and the new techniques acquired by their Moslem comrades, help to explain the heavy toll taken of English shipping in the first two decades of the century. An official report speaks of no less than 466 British ships being seized by the Algerians, and their crews reduced to slavery, between 1609 and 1616.[13] In the latter year, Sir Francis Cottington wrote to the duke of Buckingham from his embassy in Madrid to complain that English ships attempting to trade with Spain had been captured or driven ashore, and reported that the Spanish Government had sounded him out as to whether King James would consider taking some concerted action against the corsairs. The latter considered all Christians alike to be their enemies, the Spaniards argued, and since the English now had the greatest stake in the peaceful development of trade, they were likely to be the chief sufferers.[14]

These arguments carried some weight in London, and in the following year the Lords of the Council met to consider what should be done. Sir William Monson who, as Admiral of the Narrow Seas, had had some experience of suppressing piracy in the Channel, was asked for his opinion. He replied that, in his view, an expedition to destroy Algiers and stamp out Barbary piracy once and for all would not be a matter of six months but of several years. England, Holland and Spain should together provide the ships for joint operations, but the other maritime countries and cities of Europe ought to contribute to the enterprise since they too would stand to gain from its success. The king of France should at least forbid his subjects to trade with Algiers as they had been doing. It was essential to accumulate adequate supplies and equipment, to have secure bases from which to operate, and to reach full agreement from the outset on plans and command. Secrecy was essential, 'for there being several Englishmen who have been too busy in trading with pirates and furnishing them with powder and other necessities, it is to be feared that these same Englishmen will endeavour to give the Pirates intelligence'. All Turks and Moors captured should be enslaved, and special care taken not to release or ransom any who were seamen, 'for taking away their sailors, they cannot set a ship to sea, and we know their numbers cannot be great, because it is not above 12 years since the English taught them the use of navigation'. As for the renegades or Europeans who had voluntarily served the corsairs, they should be executed immediately—'for the Terror of others—for if Christian sailors can be kept from them, their piracy will cease, which otherwise will prove a great detriment to the Christian community'. The admiral finished by realistically enumerating all the obstacles—bad weather, logistical difficulties, harassment by local tribesmen, and so on—likely to add to the difficulties of an expedition.[15]

The war party, spurred on by Gondomar, Spain's influential ambassador, nevertheless pressed for action. It had the support of the earl of Nottingham, the Lord High Admiral, and of his successor Buckingham, who saw in the enterprise a chance of glory. The Levant Company favoured it, so long as it did not prejudice their trade by offending the sultan, and offered a contribution. There was persistent clamour, too, from the families of those who languished in the Barbary bagnios, so that the king 'was moved to compassionate their calamities, and resolved to endeavour to redress this public grievance'.

Monson's radical but realistic proposals were watered down to a somewhat shaky understanding with the Spaniards, the use of whose ports would prove indispensable, and the dispatch of an expedition the purpose of which was not the capture or complete destruction of Algiers, but its neutralizing as the centre of corsair activity. The new allies had not overcome their mutual distrust to the point of wishing to see the other installed in a strategic North African port. The command of the expedition was given to Sir Robert Mansell, some of whose captains had the advantage of familiarity with the Barbary coast. One had plied the trade of a privateer in the Mediterranean, whilst another had been a captive in Algiers. Mansell's squadron consisted of six ships and two pinnaces of the king's navy, with a dozen stout vessels suitably fitted out, and its complement totalled 511 guns and 2,670 men. It was the first English naval force to enter the Mediterranean. After calling at Spanish ports, the squadron arrived off Algiers at the end of November 1620 and an envoy was sent ashore to demand reparation for the damage done to British interests, the restitution of 150 ships taken in the course of the last six years and the handing over of all His Majesty's subjects—whether slaves, renegades or freed men. The Pasha, after protestations of friendship and much parley   sent aboard forty captives who he claimed were the only Englishmen in the city. Mansell had been joined by a Spanish squadron, but the winter weather now forced the allied fleet to withdraw. The following May he returned, bombarded the city, and sent in fireships in a bid to destroy all shipping in the harbour. The attempt failed, and learning from two Genoese slaves who succeeded in swimming out to his ships that the Algerians had made the port secure from further attack by closing it with a boom, he considered that he could do no more and sailed home. Almost at once the corsairs took the offensive again, seizing British ships and harrying the Spanish coast.

In 1621 Sir Thomas Roe was appointed ambassador to Constantinople, with instructions to induce the Grand Signior to call to order the piratical Regencies which nominally recognized his authority. A member of his embassy staff, accompanied by a high Ottoman official, was sent to Tunis and secured the restoration of some captured English merchandise and the release of fourteen slaves, though another score remained unransomed through lack of funds. Negotiations with Algiers proved more difficult, but agreement was eventually reached for the ransoming of 800 captives. The total number of Englishmen held as slaves throughout all the Barbary states, according to a proclamation issued by Parliament in June 1624, was around 1,500. An appeal was made to the public to give generously towards their release; the Peers set an example by each contributing £2 and members of the Commons £1.[16] The Levant Company's factor, James Frizell, was appointed consul in Algiers and showed himself particularly zealous on the captives' behalf. But relations with the Barbary states rapidly deteriorated again, and an Algerian embassy sent to England with an assortment of lions and other exotic gifts did little to mend matters. Incidents involving infractions of the peace were soon being reported from both sides. Fresh captives were taken, and the plight of those who remained unransomed grew worse. Many were dying of plague or penury, the consul reported, and not a few had abjured their faith. Two hundred and forty had been restored to freedom at the cost of £1,800, which he had been forced to raise at exorbitant rates on behalf of the Levant Company; unless the debt was quickly repaid, he feared he would be ruined.[17]

But the Company was now increasingly sceptical as to the prospects for any profitable trade with the Regencies and was anxious to end its commitments there and have no more to do with the captives and their troubles.

Consul Frizell continued his uphill task of negotiating the release of the captives. More than three quarters of the 800 mentioned in Roe's treaty were eventually freed largely through his efforts, though he and other English residents were themselves thrown into prison for a time by the Dey in an attempt to exact £6,000 as 'reparations' for damage allegedly suffered by an Algerian vessel when Buckingham attacked the common enemy at Cadiz in 1625. The Government and the Levant Company (who had not paid his salary for eight years) seemed quite deaf to his complaints and indifferent to the terrible plight of his fellow countrymen whom he was endeavouring to free, he declared, at his own expense and often at the risk of his own life. Hitherto he had supported himself through his own business, but his debts were on the point of over-whelming him. He implored the Government to consider the desperate situation of the captives, 340 of whom had been brought in during 1632 alone, and of himself. The Privy Council read the consul's report and instructed the Secretary to confer with the Levant Company for the redemption of the slaves. Nothing happened, and the consul addressed a final petition direct to the king, on his own behalf and on that of the hundreds of English slaves who looked to His Majesty for hope of redemption.[18]

The Flemish captive d'Aranda, whose adventures we have already followed, paints a picture of unrelieved wretchedness and demoralization on the part of the Englishmen imprisoned with him in the Algiers bagnios at this time. They seemed, he observed, less capable than any other nation of the art of survival. They lacked all feelings of solidarity with other prisoners, or even amongst themselves. The Turks thought so poorly of them that they would pay only 60–70 patagons for an English slave, whereas an Italian or Spaniard would fetch between 150 and 200. During one winter, he had seen more than a score of them die 'out of sheer destitution'.[19] Yet we hear too of some remarkable cases of fortitude and resourceful-ness. There was William Okeley, for example, who secretly built a tiny boat on which he and four of his friends made a successful escape (see p. 79). Another captive was a Church of England clergyman, the Reverend Devereux Spratt, who had been taken by corsairs in the Irish Channel.[20] Since Okeley and his fellow prisoners recognized him to be 'a person of very sober, grave and religious deportment', they approached him and 'humbly entreated we might enjoy the benefit of his Ministry'. Though some English merchants in Leghorn were already negotiating his ransom, the good parson stayed on for some years in Algiers in order to serve his countrymen as they had requested. His Moslem master was persuaded, through a monthly payment subscribed by the captives, to allow him a certain freedom, and sixty to eighty of them would gather in a cellar where 'twice a week this godly, painful servant of Jesus Christ prayed with us and preached the word of God'.[21]

One of the most remarkable instances of daring ingenuity comes from Tunis where the French traveller Coppin chanced to meet in the street an Englishman whom he had known in Marseilles. This man told him that he had been engaged as a valet by an English lord who was travelling abroad 'to escape the troubles of his country'. It must have been a case of from the frying pan into the fire, for both were taken by corsairs. They just had time, however, to agree that they would change stations, the master passing himself off as the valet and the valet as the master. Coppin's friend had the best of the bargain at first, for he was well treated and excused from work in expectation of the arrival of his ransom, whereas the purported valet was sent to toil in the galleys where he 'nobly bore his sufferings'. In time a Tunisian merchant received instructions from England to disburse a sum for the 'lord's' ransom, but as this was not considered enough by his owner, the 'valet' was released for 500 piastres and allowed to return to London to raise the extra 2,000 demanded. When the ruse was discovered, the master's rage was vented on the false lord, who was loaded with chains and beaten so mercilessly that it was a wonder he survived. But he too was eventually freed, after his master's anger had cooled, on the promise of another 500 piastres. He was waiting for this sum to arrive when Coppin—who unfortunately does not record the name of either his friend or the English milord—heard the story of his adventures.[22]

Distractions at home, as king and Parliament moved towards their fatal confrontation, made any consistent policy towards the problem of the Barbary corsairs difficult. In 1628, three years after Charles I's accession, when it was still hoped that Roe's treaty might provide a solution, a royal proclamation was issued calling on His Majesty's subjects to refrain from any acts of violence against the persons or shipping of Algiers, Tunis, Tetuan or Sallee.[23] It was also proposed that the Government should appoint consuls to each of those places and prohibit all privateering at their expense. But four years later, following the growing insolence of the corsair depredations, this policy of appeasement had given place to a bellicose attitude, and Roe himself was amongst those urging that 'the King grant Commission to make full prize of all the shipps and subjects of Algiers, Tunis and Sallee without any duty to the Admiralty and to sell them as slaves; to land in any part of their dominions to waste burne and spoyle; to take women and children and doe to them as they have done unto us'.[24] Other schemes were put forward which appealed even more blatantly to the passions of revenge and cupidity. One anonymous petition presented to Parliament put the blame on the Jews, since they chiefly financed the corsairs' activities and were their main beneficiaries, and argued that English merchants should recoup themselves for their losses out of the estates of Jews in England. The plight of those actually in slavery sometimes tended to be overlooked. A commission called on to consider the problem recommended that the best solution would be to recall the ambassador from the Porte and issue letters of marque; but that it would be unwise even to consider ransoming the captives since that would only encourage the corsairs to persist in their nefarious trade.[25]

But something clearly had to be done. Though Algiers and England remained nominally at peace, the corsairs grew increasingly bold in their raids. 1631 saw the descent on Baltimore and the enslavement of its population of Irish fisherfolk by the rascally Dutch renegade Morat Raïs. Five years later the shipowners of Exeter, Plymouth, Dartmouth and other places in the West Country were petitioning the Lords of the Council and complaining that the pirates, piloted through the English Channel by Irish or English captives, had become so numerous and terrible that it was unsafe to put to sea and the fishermen could no longer ply their trade. A similar complaint was made by the Deputy Lieutenant of Cornwall who estimated the number of pirate ships as at least sixty. In 1640 the Mayor of Plymouth reported the despoiling of the *Elizabeth* and of many smaller vessels by three Turkish raiders off the Lizard.[26] A newsletter of the same year declared that the 'roguish pirates', who kept out of sight of the king's ships by day and descended on the coast at night, had recently carried off sixty men, women and children near St Michael's Mount.[27] Petitions poured into the Court and Parliament. One, of 3 October 1640, spoke of no less than 3,000 English wretches

in miserable captivity, undergoing divers and most insufferable labour, such as rowing in galleys, drawing carts, grinding in mills, with divers such unchristianlike work most lamentable to express, and most burdensome to undergo, withal suffering much hunger and many blows on their bare bodies, by which cruelty many, not being able to undergo it, have been forced to turn Mohammedans.[28]

Collections were made throughout the kingdom for the relief and ransoming of the captive Englishmen, but the problem had now grown beyond the scope of private charity. In 1641 Parliament induced the king to earmark a percentage of the customs dues—the 'Algerian duty'—for the financing of naval expeditions and the redemption of captives in Barbary. With the money thus made available some captives were freed, and in 1646 Edmund Casson arrived in Algiers as Parliament's envoy and ransomed another 244 men, women and children out of the 750 estimated to be in Algerian hands. The basic price agreed upon, including customs dues, was £38 a head, but some captives, specially the women, proved far more expensive. Elizabeth Mancor of Dundee cost £200, Sarah Riply of London £800, Mary Riply with her two children £1,000, Alice Hayes of Edinburgh £1,100, Thomas Thomson of London £1,300 and Mary Bruster of Youghal £1,392. Casson continued his work until his death in Algiers eight years later, by which time it had cost the treasury the considerable sum of nearly £40,000. A new treaty, optimistically intended to remain in force 'until the end of the world', was concluded which provided for the resumption of normal trade and stipulated that no Englishman was to be bought or sold as a slave, and no English captives taken by the rovers of Tunis, Sallee or Tripoli brought into Algiers for disposal.[29]

Tunis concluded no treaty with England and was soon the scene of fresh trouble. The *Princess*, returning from Zante with a cargo of currants, was seized and her crew enslaved, allegedly as a reprisal for similarly hostile British actions. Cromwell instructed Admiral Blake to demand the restitution of the ship, its cargo and crew. Restitution was refused, as was his request to take on water and provisions—an act of defiance which cost the Bey the destruction of nine vessels anchored off Port Farina. Fresh from this brilliant, if somewhat barren, exploit, Blake proceeded to Algiers, where the Dey understandably hastened to give him a more friendly reception, furnishing him with the supplies needed by the fleet, confirming and slightly amplifying the provisions of Casson's treaty, and ransoming twenty-seven Englishmen who found themselves in captivity there regardless of the assurances given that no British subjects were to be enslaved. But within two years, despite Blake's show of force, relations with Algiers had deteriorated once more. The Dey wrote to Cromwell complaining of 'treachery and falsehood' on the part of the English, whose ships, he alleged, transported the subjects and cargoes of hostile states, served under enemy flags, connived at the misuse of their passes by foreign vessels, and handed over Moslems to their enemies.

To stop these alleged abuses the corsairs advanced a claim which was to remain a constant bone of contention—the right to search British ships. Lord Winchelsea, His Majesty's ambassador to Constantinople, stopped at Algiers to conclude a treaty confirming the peace but admitting the Algerians' right to take off enemy foreigners and their goods from British ships. This clause was repudiated by the king's ministers and Lord Sandwich was instructed to force the corsairs to drop the unacceptable claim. He failed. 'My Lord hath not done what he went for,' his kinsman Pepys commented ruefully, 'the want of money puts all things, and above all the Navy, out of order.'[30] Sir John Lawson, who succeeded him in command of the squadron, negotiated a compromise by which the Algerians were authorized to stop British vessels and inspect their passes; but even if no passes were produced the ships were not to be interfered with if the majority of their crew were clearly British. Such vague and unsatisfactory guide-lines, even if the corsairs had any intention of abiding by them, inevitably gave rise to trouble. The Divan brushed aside protests by asserting that any hostile acts must have been the work of individual captains, 'for which we have drowned one, banished another; some have fled to escape our justice, and divers have been imprisoned'. The war went on; Sir Edward Spragge sent in fireships and burned an Algerian squadron under the guns of Bougie, provoking a mutiny of the janissaries who turned on their Agha and murdered him. But hostilities were confused and inconclusive, costing the English—according to Robert Cole, later consul at Algiers—the loss of 157 merchant ships, some 3,000 seamen and about £300,000.[31]

It was, as usual, the unfortunate captives who suffered most. Harrowing petitions continued to reach the king. One captive described how he was 'made daily to grind a mill as a horse with a chain upon each legge, and as an addition to his misery he is almost starved with hunger, besides other grossest usage'. Much of the Redemption Fund raised by the Algiers Duty was appropriated for other purposes. The bishops raised a fund of their own and sent two clergymen to Algiers to see that it was well spent. Charitable merchants like William Bowtell of London and his factor Lionel Crofts courted financial disaster in their efforts to arrange ransoms. In a petition for reimbursement presented to the Council we find Bowtell listing the difficulties encountered and the losses incurred. For each captive ransomed £40 had been promised by the Government. Crofts had ransomed 391 captives, though for sums far higher than the official bounty, and for some of them not even that had been paid. Ransom prices had risen 50%, and since the treaties in force failed to include the usual stipulation that slaves should be redeemed at the price originally paid for them their masters were asking whatever they liked. Persons of rank were ruinously expensive and often lax about repaying money advanced on their behalf. The newly appointed governor of Carolina, for instance, had been captured *en route* for his post and later ransomed for £375; but Bowtell only succeeded in recovering £120 of this sum from him. The Dey held two English slaves, John Cave and Joseph Gill, for whom he demanded £250; as Bowtell had only the bounty of £40 a head from public funds he was left £170 out of pocket over the deal. Some captives had been redeemed and then died from plague before they could refund the cost of their ransoms. Finally, Bowtell's factor Crofts had died as the result of his exertions. A ship with a cargo valued at £2,500 which Bowtell had sent out to be sold in order to raise money for ransoms had been seized and auctioned in order to pay Crofts' debts, so that not a single captive had benefited.[32]

Pressure for the ransoming of captives seems, paradoxically, to have come less from their countrymen than from their captors. We find the Dey of Algiers peremptorily demanding that action should be taken before the end of November 1674 to complete their redemption—'the first and chief poynt of our Peace'—and the impecunious Charles II reluctantly responding.[33] Not only was the Dey himself eager to tap this source of revenue, but the private slave-owners were impatient to realize their human assets. This seemed to them the more urgent since Algiers' relations with France were steadily deteriorating. The Barbary states had their own fashion of deciding matters of peace and war. They could not afford to be too much at peace and so see the flow of prizes and prisoners dwindle; neither, on the other hand, could they risk hostilities with too many powerful nations at once. By the beginning of 1682 Algiers was at war with France and so ready for effective peace with England. The treaty concluded that year by Admiral Herbert,[34] whilst declaring the enslavement of His Majesty's subjects, or the sale of those already reduced to slavery, to be illegal, left many matters unsatisfactorily vague. Corsair ships might board British merchantmen to inspect the official passes which they were required to carry, though no violence was to be used and no persons of other nationality might be taken off. English slaves at present in Algerian hands were to be redeemed, not at their original market price (as stipulated in Casson's treaty), but for 'such reasonable sums as any slaves of other nations usually pay when they are redeemed'—a sure recipe, as Consul Frizell had discovered, for acrimonious haggling.

Nor should the Dey or any other slave-owner be forced to free
them if unwilling to do so, or His Majesty obliged to redeem
them within any given time; the transaction was clearly
envisaged as one of mutual convenience between the con-
tracting parties, whilst the rights and interests of the slaves
themselves remained a secondary consideration. Father Le
Vacher, soon to end his life at the cannon's mouth, may not
have been motivated solely by anti-English prejudice when he
stigmatized the treaty as purchasing 'the most shameful peace
imaginable'.[35]

For all its shortcomings and the infractions which almost
immediately started to occur, the 1682 treaty was several times
renewed and amended; it also prompted similar agreements
with Tunis and Tripoli. Twelve years later the English consul
reported that none of His Majesty's subjects, who had been
taken under the British flag, remained captive in any of the
three Regencies, with the exception of one who refused his
liberty.[36] Slavery was still the fate reserved for Englishmen
whose captors could invoke some loophole in the treaties or
who ignored the authority of Deys and Beys. Not a few of these
unfortunates regained their freedom thanks to the generosity
of William Betton, a wealthy London ironmonger who died in
1724 and left his fortune in trust for this purpose.[37] We hear of
the consul drawing on this fund to ransom thirteen Englishmen
who had been wrecked in 1808 near Djidjelli and enslaved by
Kabyles who cared little or nothing for any treaty. By and
large, however, peace of a sort between England and the
Barbary states was preserved for a hundred years and more.

Morocco, during much of the seventeenth century, also
successfully disproved the boast that Britons never, never shall
be slaves. At first, such relations as existed between the two
countries were good. In Elizabeth's reign they were drawn
together through trade and a common hatred of Spain.
Edmund Hogan, the queen's ambassador, was given a friendly
reception in 1577 by Sultan 'Abd al-Malik and optimistically
reported that 'he beareth a greater affection to our nation than
to others because of our religion, which forbiddeth worship of
Idols, and the Moores call him the Christian King'.[38] England,
it is true, was also allied to Morocco's enemy Portugal, and
English volunteers served in the ranks of King Sebastian's

ill-fated army at Alcázarquivir. But Portugal's defeat opened up fresh commercial opportunities for England, who traded her woollens for Moroccan gold, leather, sugar and saltpetre. A wider alliance was even envisaged for ambitious joint operations against Spain but came to nothing after the deaths of Elizabeth and al-Manzur, 'Abd al-Malik's successor.[39] Morocco then declined into a period of anarchy and civil war, which allowed the emergence on the Atlantic coast of a new centre of piratical power which rapidly became the scourge of English shipping. In August 1625, 800 Englishmen were reported to be held at Sallee, and a year later the number had risen to 1,500. We find a petition presented that year to Buckingham on behalf of the distressed wives of 'almost 2,000 poor mariners remaining most miserable captives at Sallee' begging the favourite to intercede for them with the king.[40]

A large proportion of the corsair ships infesting the sea approaches and raiding the coasts of England in the 1630s and 1640s came from Sallee. Occasionally captured seamen succeeded in dramatically turning the tables on the corsairs, as in February 1626 when five Englishmen brought a Sallee ship into Cookhaven claiming that they had slain no less than sixty-two of their captors![41] Three months later, another corsair vessel was brought into Looe with thirty-two Moslems below hatches.[42] But so long as the raiders could make use of friendly Flemish bases and continue to outsail the English warships sent against them, little could be done to stop their harassment; it looked likely, as one frustrated admiral put it, that 'these picaroons will lie hankering upon the coast, unless it be resolved to sack Sallee, which some report easy to perform'.[43]

But appeasement, as formulated in the 1628 proclamation forbidding hostile acts against the Barbary states (see p. 140), was meanwhile the order of the day. This allowed some merchants to do profitable trade with Sallee, though the risks were great. One petition to the king complains that an English privateer seized a Sallee ship and sold its contents and crew to the Spaniards, 'whereupon our merchants' goods and their factors in Sallee are embargoed and divers ships taken and Englishmen made slaves'.[44] The Government dispatched its agent, Captain John Harrison, on several visits to Sallee to ransom captives and settle such incidents. He brought with him not only money and Moslem prisoners to be exchanged, but sometimes cannon and munitions as well.[45] The folly of such dealings did not pass without protest from men like Sir Henry Marten, the eminent lawyer and Cornish Member of Parliament who saw in the Salletines 'a company of pirates with whom there is no treaty or confederacy'.[46] Occasionally a captive might be restored to freedom through luck or ingenuity. We read of Lodowick Boyer who was freed 'by a Hamburger whom he had served for one year and a half to teach his son English and to play upon the orgarian'.[47] But the great majority had no other hope than the efforts made on their behalf by friends or government. Many, one petition complained, were ransomed but still languished in Sallee for lack of passages home.[48] Another petition, submitted on behalf of 1,000 women whose husbands had been enslaved for three years or more, lamented their 'extreme labour, want of sustenance and grievous torments'.[49] By mid-1635, when Secretary Coke made his report on England's foreign relations to the king, matters had grown so bad that he could say of the Moroccans, with bitterness if with some exaggeration, that 'the spoils of our people are their greatest wealth'.[50]

In 1637 a squadron of four ships commanded by Captain William Rainsborough was dispatched with instructions to blockade Sallee, destroy as much shipping as possible, and secure the release of all English slaves there. The previous year the Salletines had taken 500 English captives, and since their fleet had subsequently been reinforced, were anticipating a still larger haul. Rainsborough arrived just in time to prevent the corsairs sailing, though some hundreds of English slaves had already been sent to Algiers for sale.[51] At first his warships could do little damage, the fortifications being strong and 'the Governor being an Andaluce, an obstinate fellow, puffed up with his luck in thieving'.[52] But eventually Rainsborough was able to ally himself with the leader of an opposing faction, the warlike marabout al-'Ayashi (picturesquely referred to in contemporary accounts as the Saint of Old Sallee) and in return obtained the release of between 3–400 captive men, women and children.

After Rainsborough's expedition, the curious alternation of

trade, piracy and truce was gradually resumed. During the reign of Muley Ismael English captives, like those of other European nations, were sent to join his labour force at Meknes and sometimes impressed into his armies. Miners were much in demand as sappers, and we hear of three of them eventually given their freedom as a reward for their services in under-mining enemy fortifications.[53] One of the imperial executioners was a butcher from Exeter.[54] Francis Brooks, captured in 1681 and held for ten years, gives the number of his enslaved countrymen as 340, whilst Thomas Phelps, captured three years after him, puts it at 260.[55] In 1720 Commodore Stewart arrived with instructions from George I to conclude a peace treaty, and ransom all the king's subjects. He succeeded in freeing 296, two dozen of whom were ships' masters. But for those who had abjured their religion and entered the sultan's services he could do nothing; one was a Cornish lad, Thomas Pellow, who managed to escape twenty-three years later after many adventures. When, following Muley Ismael's death, Consul-General Russell sought from his heir a renewal and confirmation of the peace with England, he was able only to discover and release two English slaves—one who had been taken whilst serving on a Dutch ship, and another who had been a great favourite with the queen and been concealed by her when the other slaves were handed over. An Englishman who accompanied Russell and published an account of his mission declares that the conditions of the Christian slaves had improved since Muley Ismael's day, and that 'they lived much better in Barbary than ever they did in their own country'.[56] He compared their bagnio favourably with an English prison, and maintained that some possessed mules and even servants of their own, whilst 'many have carried considerable sums out of the country'. It is difficult to give much credence to this rosy picture, which is in sharp contrast to the grim experiences recorded not long afterwards by other Englishmen who had the misfortune to taste of Moroccan slavery (see p. 151).

From Corsairs to Colonialists

The eighteenth century saw a decline in the Barbary corsairs' activities and in the number of the Christians they enslaved. Europe's two leading naval and commercial powers, Britain and France, had become too strong to be harassed with impunity, and the predators found it wiser to look for smaller prey. Neither Paris nor London objected to this state of affairs. Each saw advantage in making its own terms with the corsairs, either by imposing its will or buying them off, in the expectation that they would do more harm to its rivals. The smaller trading nations like Holland, Sweden and Denmark, whose ships were becoming too numerous in the Mediterranean for the liking of Britain and France, would suffer the most. Except for Venice, which continued to deal some shrewd blows down to the eve of the Republic's own extinction, the Italian states were incapable of preventing the toll in booty and captives which the Barbary marauders continued to take. Spain, once Christendom's chief bulwark, now scarcely counted as a serious factor. Her final bid, in 1775, to send an armada against Algiers ended in disaster, and all but a few of her *presidios* had become military and administrative liabilities which she was ready to barter for commercial privileges.

The size of the corsair fleets dwindled. Plague and famine periodically decimated the population, carrying off 17,000 from Algiers in 1787 alone and reducing the inhabitants to a mere 30,000 by the end of the century. The bagnios suffered particularly from these visitations; in 1740 the beylik slaves mustered no more than 442.[1] Despite the higher ransoms demanded for them, the drop in revenue from reduced sales meant difficulty in paying the janissaries and consequently more frequent riots and revolts. Tribute continued to be collected by armed columns sent regularly against the tribes of the interior, for though the ties which bound them to

Constantinople were now flimsy, the Regencies remained lands under foreign military occupation. Energies were also frittered away in constant feuding between Algiers and Tunis. The former, when strong enough to be aggressive, still nourished ambitions too at the expense of Morocco, but that country, even more backward and isolated from European contacts, kept aloof from eastern entanglements. The industrial revolution, which was beginning to transform the face of Europe, sent scarcely a ripple to the shores of North Africa. The seizure of prizes and the enslavement of captives remained an essential if anachronistic prop of its still primitive economies.

Algiers, the strongest of the Barbary states, was ruled despotically by its Deys, successors to the 'Triennial Pashas' previously appointed by the Porte for three-year terms of office. In the seventeenth century, power passed to the Divan, the unruly assembly composed of the Agha of the Janissaries and other military chiefs who made and unmade the Deys. The Ottoman Pasha was at first retained as a figure-head, but in 1710 the title was assumed by the Dey, who thus became the nominal, as well as the real, ruler of the Regency. But though exercising arbitrary and absolute power, the Dey was himself in a sense no freer than his own slaves. He lived constantly under the threat of assassination. Nearly half of the thirty or so Deys in power in Algiers between 1671 and 1818 took office after first killing their predecessors.

Tunis evolved a rather more satisfactory system of virtual hereditary monarchy under the Husainid Beys, who emerged to power during the struggle against Algiers. Though distracted by bitter intra-dynastic disputes, they gave the country a more stable and enlightened government, and some rulers fostered agriculture and commerce, carried out public works and favoured the development of a cultural life based on orthodox Moslem law. But the foundation of their power remained an efficient Turkish army (though under Tunisian, not Ottoman, control) and their fleet of corsair ships.

Tripoli was similarly ruled by its Qaramanli dynasty, successors of the great corsair chief Dragut and the Ottoman Pashas. The Qaramanlis achieved too a certain success in combining the encouragement of commerce with the practice of piracy. But Tripoli retained closer links with Constantinople, and when the corsairs had had their day it was not the European colonialists, quarrelling as to whether a French or a British protégé should claim the inheritance, but the ailing Ottoman empire which managed for a time to extend its sway over the country.

Morocco preserved a political system which had changed even less than those of the other Barbary states. In the course of the seventeenth century, the Moroccans succeeded in eliminating the European enclaves on its Atlantic coast, though not those (with the exception of Tangier, evacuated by England in 1684) in the Mediterranean. The Sallee Rovers continued to harass Atlantic shipping, despite British reprisals and the gradual silting up of their protective sandbanks. The State had a direct stake in the continuance of piracy, since the sultan owned half of the corsair ships as well as taking a high percentage of the profits made by the remainder. Muley Ismael's death in 1727 was followed by alternating periods of anarchy and harsh despotic rule. Even when their country was nominally at peace with the Moroccans, Europeans who fell into their hands through shipwreck or other misfortunes could expect the traditional treatment meted out to slaves, as we learn from the account left by survivors from the *Inspector*, wrecked in the Bay of Tangier in 1746 and reduced to the verge of cannibalism in a *mazmorra* before being put to forced labour on the sultan's fortifications.[2] Morocco remained closed to outside influences until the 1830s, when there were still less than 300 European residents to be found throughout its huge territory. It was not until the French had occupied Algiers and showed signs of threatening Morocco that the latter began to move out of her isolation and look to protection from Britain, who favoured Moroccan independence as a check to Spanish or French designs on Gibraltar and as a new field for her trade.

Thanks to her treaties, 'presents', badly needed supplies of war material and the occasional show of force, England protected her commerce in the Mediterranean and maintained tolerable relations with the Barbary states. But there remained grounds in plenty for friction, and not a few of His Britannic Majesty's subjects still fell victim to the traditional system of enslavement and extortion on which, though now less heavily, the Barbary states continued to rely. The principle that no

British subject should be enslaved, bought or sold in the Algerian domains was confirmed by successive treaties, but the Deys showed inexhaustible ingenuity and persistence in devising ways of evading the undertaking. One argued that any captive taken from an enemy ship and claiming to be a British subject should produce a certificate to this effect, under the seal and hand of the monarch himself to prove it. When the consul expostulated that no sovereign concerned himself with such minor matters, which were left to His Majesty's consuls to settle, the men concerned were sent to join the bagnio labour gangs.[3] The right of asylum on British warships also gave rise to frequent complaints. To avoid such embarrassing incidents, visiting men-of-war were expected to stand well out to sea, and some even remained under sail whilst waiting to deliver and receive consular correspondence. Even so, slaves occasionally managed to swim out to them and escape. In 1773, the Dey attempted to extort an undertaking from the captain of the *Alarm* that any such fugitives should be delivered up, and when Fraser, the English consul, supported the captain's refusal, he was declared *persona non grata* and expelled. Though later sent back under the guns of a British squadron, the Dey still refused to receive him, and the British Government tamely appointed another consul in his place.[4]

The sometimes considerable number of British subjects taken whilst serving under a foreign, generally Spanish, flag also presented problems. Many fell into Algerian hands after deserting from Oran, others were amongst the garrison captured when the *presidio* fell in 1732.[5] They met at first with little sympathy from the consul, who refused to recognize them as any longer subjects of the Crown. Ambrose Stanyford, who took over the consulate in 1741, was touched by their continuing plight and urged on his government the desirability of ransoming them, which he believed could be done for as little as £25–30 a head in view of the glut of slaves on the market. Another influx of captives whose nationality was in question occurred in 1747, when a detachment of the Hibernian Regiment, which had been serving with the Spanish forces in Italy, was captured on its way back to Spain. It included one lieutenant-colonel, six captains, ten subalterns and sixty privates, together with a number of wives and children.[6]

We have already seen the tragic and dramatic fate which befell one mother and her child (see pp. 40–1).

Much depended on the degree of sympathy shown by the consul for such unfortunates with a dubious call on his protection, and also on his personal standing with the Dey and with the British merchant community. With the latter relations were sometimes strained, for their interests could be widely at variance. The consul might think it his duty to demand the restitution of a prize, whilst the merchants hoped to see it condemned so that they could buy its contents at bargain prices. The consul would hesitate to issue a ship with a clean bill of health if there was any taint of plague in the city, whilst the merchants would resent the loss occasioned by a long stay in quarantine at its port of destination. The slaves themselves sometimes found themselves caught up in such conflicts of interest. In 1745 a vessel loaded with goods consigned to the merchant John Ford was shipwrecked on the Algerian coast and its captain and crew enslaved by the Kabyles, over whom the Dey could exercise little control. Intermediaries came to Algiers with exorbitant ransom demands: 60 golden sequins for the captain, 52 for the mate, and 48 (four times the usual price) for each sailor. The consul, aware that compliance would create a dangerous precedent and send up all ransom demands, refused to pay these rates and held out for a release on reasonable terms. Ford, meanwhile, had raised a public subscription amongst his friends and paid over the 60 sequins asked for the captain, and so made it impossible to get the others freed at less than the price demanded for them.[7] The fact that the consul himself was often appointed from the ranks of the merchant community—Ford himself later succeeded to the office—was hardly calculated to eliminate the basic conflict of interests or ensure high standards of disinterested public service.

The outbreak of war between Britain and revolutionary France in 1793 gave a fresh stimulus to corsair activity in the Mediterranean. The two European powers, long rivals for commercial advantage and political influence, were now more than ever anxious to court the Barbary states as allies, or at least as friendly neutrals. France, moreover, was soon to need immense quantities of North African grain with which to feed her armies, and there were rich profits to be made from cargoes which slipped through Britain's continental blockade. In 1797, Napoleon put an end to the Republic of Venice, whose fleets had so long warred against the Porte and its Barbary auxiliaries. The following year he captured Malta, Christendom's traditional base for operations against the corsairs. But his invasion of Egypt involved him in hostilities with Turkey, who brought pressure to bear on the Regencies to declare war on France. They did so half-heartedly, contenting themselves with interning or expelling French subjects, and making peace again in 1800. The following year, renewed pressure from Turkey and Britain forced Algiers to resume hostilities, and early in 1801 Tunis followed suit. But whatever their formal status in the war, the Barbary states could only profit from the European convulsion, and their ships were soon not only infesting the Mediterranean and harrying the islands and coasts of Italy with impunity, but preying upon shipping in the Atlantic.

A new name had already been added to the corsairs' list of tributary states. Once Britain's American colonies had won independence they ceased to enjoy the protection of her navy. The first American prizes were taken and American captives brought back to Algiers in July 1785. Some perished in the bagnios from plague and other diseases. One young sailor, accused of stealing fruit from the Dey's garden where he had been put to work, lost his reason after been given the bastinado. Others were more fortunate. Two bought their freedom, with the help of Jewish brokers, at the cost of 2,000 Mexican dollars a head. Another, James Cathcart, rose to become the Dey's Chief Christian Secretary. Whilst fresh batches of American captives continued to be brought in, the President of the United States and his advisers had to face the shocking fact that their fellow citizens were being enslaved and that steps must be taken to effect their release and protect others from suffering the same fate. In February 1797 eighty-two surviving captives arrived back in Philadelphia. The payment of their ransoms, 'presents' to the Dey and the first instalment of an annual tribute in the shape of naval stores, cost the youthful republic nearly one million dollars.[8]

The success of the Dey of Algiers in tapping this new source of transatlantic revenue stirred the rulers of Tripoli and Tunis to emulation. The latter promptly seized the *Eliza* of Boston and only released her crew on payment of 10,000 dollars. Peter Lyle, an English renegade in the service of the Bey of Tripoli, intercepted the *Betsy* and the *Sophia*, but had to release the latter when she was found to be carrying American bullion to the Dey of Algiers whom the Bey did not dare offend.[9] Cathcart, and another ex-captive Richard O'Brien, both now holding consular office, did what they could to moderate the clamorous demands of the Barbary rulers, whilst public opinion in the United States grew increasingly indignant, particularly after 1801 when Tripolitanian corsairs seized several American ships. 'Millions for defence—not one cent for tribute' became a popular slogan. In 1803 two American ships were commissioned to strike back by blockading Tripoli. One, the *Philadelphia*, ran aground and was captured with its crew of 307—a setback partially redeemed by the daring exploit of a boarding party which fired the prize before it could by recommissioned by the enemy. The following year an American squadron returned to bombard Tripoli and compel the Bey, who was demanding ransoms to the tune of three million dollars, to exchange prisoners and to cease from further molestation of American shipping, though Washington nevertheless agreed to pay him a small sum in 'compensation'. In 1812, impatient over the delay in receiving the annual tribute, Algiers expelled the American consul and declared war. Three years later, after Raïs Hamidou, the last of her great corsair captains, had been defeated and killed in action against a squadron of eight American warships, the Dey was compelled to agree to the restoration of all American captives and property and to drop all further demands for tribute.

The smaller European powers were treated with equal insolence and with less danger of retaliation. In 1808, the Dey of Algiers, irritated by Denmark's delay in producing the customary tribute, ordered the consul, a retired admiral, to be seized and sent in chains to the bagnio. The following day he was driven out to forced labour with the other slaves and only released as the result of a collective protest by the consular corps. The Dutch consul was treated in much the same way and for the same reason, and was threatened with having his wife and children auctioned off as slaves unless the tribute from his country was promptly paid.[10] Italy, vulnerable as ever, was raided almost as savagely as in the days of Barbarossa. In 1798 a thousand Tunisian corsairs descended on the island of San Pietro and carried off an almost equal number of captives. Three-quarters of them were redeemed five years later, the remainder having died, apostatized, or been sold or ransomed privately. Though several heads of state, including Tsar Alexander I of Russia, intervened on behalf of the captives, their release was chiefly due to one man whom no corsair dared offend—Napoleon.[11] It seemed at one time, after he had gained control of the Two Sicilies, that the emperor's designs might include a decisive blow against Algiers, and orders were given for appropriate preliminary plans to be made. But political and military developments diverted his attention elsewhere; Algiers was to have twenty years' respite from French expansionist ambitions.

The power of Napoleon's chief adversary, even before achieving victory in the long struggle, also remained formidable enough to cause the Barbary rulers to treat Britain with circumspection. In 1814 the British consul in Tripoli, Warrington, had a corsair captain hanged from the mast of a British ship he had imprudently seized.[12] The narrative of Filippo Pananti, captured the year before by Raïs Hamidou, illustrates the influence then wielded by His Britannic Majesty's representative in Algiers.[13] Although he had been living in England for a number of years, Pananti was an Italian. The consul nevertheless had him released without ransom, together with another Italian who had married an Englishwoman. No wonder the grateful captive describes him as 'one of those men who do honour to humanity'. An account of Pananti's adventures was published in England and prompted reflections on the part of the naval captain who translated them which indicate the trend of thinking in England at the close of the Napoleonic wars. It seemed both astonishing and shameful that European civilians were still being seized and reduced to slavery in the Mediterranean by 'a set of monsters who vie with one another in the deepest and bitterest hostility towards Christianity and civilization'. The monsters, moreover, happened to inhabit a particularly favoured part of Africa whose acquisition 'would at once throw open the whole of that vast continent and lead to its speedy civilization'. Its conquest would not be easy, but 'expeditions sent to the coast of North Africa will not only be paid for by the treasures which abound there, but each individual concerned may safely calculate on being enriched for the remainder of his life'—a singularly prescient prophecy, at least as regards the leaders of the expedition launched not many years later. In conclusion, argued Pananti's naval translator, 'the great work of bringing Africa into the bosom of civilization' should be a cooperative European effort in which England, as the leading maritime and commercial power, 'should unquestionably be at its head'. The second place might however be allotted to France, 'enthusiastic, animated, fond of ardent enterprise', whilst Italy, to make amends for having suffered more than any other country, should also be given a share in the pickings.[14]

The theme, with more romantic trappings, was taken up by another Englishman—Admiral Sir Sidney Smith, famous for his defence of Acre which had blocked Napoleon's ambitions in the Near East. The establishment of a grandiose Society of Knights Liberators of the White Slaves in Africa was announced and the potentates of Europe were canvassed for their support. The admiral bombarded courts and chanceries with memoranda in which he drew attention to the damage inflicted on commerce by the Barbary corsairs and the scandal of Christian standards being continually affronted by the practice of enslaving and selling innocent men, women and children. He denounced the complicity of European governments who shamefully supplied the funds and war materials enabling the Moslem pirates to prey on other Europeans, and the need to establish a defensive organization to take up the tasks which the Knights of St John had performed from Malta in times past. He proposed the steps which should be taken; diplomatic initiatives to induce the Porte to curb the defiant Deys and Beys who still recognized its nominal suzerainty, and to deprive them, if they remained obdurate, of the support of local chieftains and of their own influential subjects. The European powers should also enforce a blockade of the Barbary coast by setting up a joint force, to which each would furnish their contingent of a maritime, or more properly speaking, amphibious force which, without compromising any flag, and without depending on the wars or the political events of the Nations, should constantly guard the shores of the Mediterranean and take upon itself the important office of watching, pursuing and capturing all pirates by land and by sea.

Finally, he offered his own services for the command of such a force.[15]

Metternich, Talleyrand, and the other statesmen who gathered at the Congress of Vienna and then at Aix-la-Chapelle to redraw the map of Europe were not the men to welcome such quixotic schemes. Nor was the British Government, when at length it decided to act, prepared to venture beyond the traditional methods of unilateral action. In 1816, Lord Exmouth was sent to the Mediterranean with a strong squadron to demand that the Ionian islanders, who had now passed under British protection, should be accorded the same immunities as British subjects, and also to oblige the Barbary states to make peace with Sardinia and Naples.

The terms negotiated by Exmouth at Algiers showed little change in the customary pattern of acquiescence in the rights claimed by the corsairs and hallowed by *usanza*. Naples was to pay Algiers an annual tribute and the usual 'presents' and to ransom Sicilian captives at 1,000 dollars a head. A deal was struck on behalf of Sardinia for half this rate, but Algerian captives were also to be handed over in part exchange. The Ionian islanders held captive in Algiers were recognized as British subjects and freed. With this partial success behind him, Exmouth sailed on to Tripoli and Tunis where he was able to overawe the rulers into releasing all Christian slaves regardless of nationality—of which there were more than 1,600 in Tunis—and signing a declaration to the effect that any captives taken in the future should be treated as prisoners of war, not as slaves. But the right of the corsairs to prey on foreign shipping was not formally renounced; indeed, it was implicitly recognized in the treaty.

Exmouth then sailed back to renew pressure on Algiers. The Divan rejected his demands that the enslavement of all

Christians should be abolished, and declared that such a drastic break with tradition could only be sanctioned at the express command of the Sublime Porte. Although the sultan's writ had long ceased to run in the Regencies, it was eventually agreed that Algerian ambassadors should be sent to Constantinople, and also to London, to discuss the question. After Exmouth's squadron had sailed off, the Dey vented his spleen by ordering the imprisonment of all Italians, now under British protection, resident in Oran. Another hundred or so Christians were set upon and murdered in Bône, and much European property was plundered. After a few months' absence, Exmouth was back before Algiers, his squadron reinforced with a number of Dutch ships. In reprisal for the massacre at Bône he ordered a massive bombardment of the Dey's city.

In the fury of the ensuing engagement the Christian slaves, the demand for whose release was a basic cause of the quarrel, found themselves in danger of being slaughtered. The Frenchman Dumont, whose thirty years' servitude in the interior and eventual transfer to Algiers we have already noted (see p. 67), has left us a slave's-eye view of the affair. 'We were all conducted, to the number of 1,500, including 30 Frenchmen, into an immense cavern at the top of the mountain of Algiers', he recalls.[16] The climb up the steep hillside took some four hours, for the slaves were all heavily chained. Exmouth's bombardment had begun, and as they watched the flames rising from the city below, their keepers fell upon them mercilessly. 'The Minister of the Dey, without taking counsel with his master,' Dumont continues, 'had given the order that all the slaves should be beheaded. Four had fallen by the scimitar when the Turks, who acted with reluctance and who come far short of the Arabs in ferocity of character, despatched one of their party to urge the Dey to put a stop to this butchery.' Before the messenger returned with orders to stop the killing, thirty more victims had been executed. His return gave the signal for a stampede to safety. 'We rushed out of the cave, and dragging our chains, pushed forward through brambles and thickets, regardless of the blood streaming from our faces and bodies. We simply did not feel our wounds any longer. Then we were taken aboard a number of English boats.'

The damage and casualties caused by the bombardment were severe, and Exmouth purchased his victory at the cost of over 800 British lives. But the Dey was forced to yield to all his demands and to affix his signature to the following historic document:

In consideration of the deep interest manifested by His Royal Highness the Prince Regent of England for the termination of Christian slavery, His Highness the Dey of Algiers, in token of his sincere desire to maintain inviolable his friendly relations with Great Britain, and to manifest his amicable disposition and high respect towards the powers of Europe, declares that, in the event of future war with any European power, not any of the prisoners shall be consigned to slavery, but treated with all humanity as prisoners of war, until regularly exchanged, according to European practice in like cases; and that at the termination of hostilities, they shall be restored to their respective countries without ransom; and the practice of condemning Christian prisoners of war to slavery is hereby formally and for ever renounced.

Done in duplicate, in the warlike city of Algiers, in the presence of Almighty God, the 28 day of August, in the year of Jesus Christ, 1816, and on the 6th day of the moon of the month Shawoal, in the year 1231 of the Hejira.[17]

Abraham Salame, the Levantine interpreter who had accompanied the expedition, was sent ashore to see to the embarkation of the liberated slaves and takes up Dumont's story:

When I arrived on shore, it was the most pitiful sight, to see all those poor creatures, in what a horrible state they were; but it is impossible to describe the joy and cheerfulness of them. When our boats came inside of the mole, I wished to receive them [the slaves] from the captain of the port, by number, but could not, because they directly began to push and throw themselves into the boats by crowds, ten or twenty persons together, so that it was impossible to count them; then I told him, that we should make an exact list of them, in order to know to what number they amounted. It was indeed a most glorious, and an ever memorably merciful act, for England, over all Europe, to see these poor slaves, when our boats were shoving with them off the shore, all at once take off their hats and exclaim, in Italian, '*Viva il Re d'Inghilterra, il padre eterno! e 'l Ammiraglio Inglese che ci ha liberato da questo secondo inferno!*' . . . and afterwards, they began to prove what they had suffered by beating their breasts, and loudly swearing at the Algerines.[18]

When the tally was taken, it was found to amount to 3,003, including the slaves released through Exmouth's efforts in Tunis and Tripoli and on his previous visit to Algiers.[19]

Despite the punishment inflicted by Exmouth's bombardment and the formal renunciation of Christian slavery, few signs of a change of heart could be detected on the part of the Barbary states. Whenever they felt strong enough, the corsairs continued to take prizes and to seize captives—'only we now call them prisoners and not slaves,' Yusuf Pasha of Tripoli is reported to have observed. If the number of attractive girls for the harem was in short supply, the Dey made do with what he could pick up in the streets of Algiers. One case—much publicized by the President of the Society of Knights Liberators of the White Slaves—created quite a stir on account of its operatic character and eventual happy ending. A pretty Sardinian girl called Rosa Ponsombia was waylaid by the Dey's henchmen whilst on the way back from a visit to the French consulate and spirited away to the harem. After some days she managed to throw down a note into the street addressed to Macdonald, the British consul, informing him of her plight and warning him of similar designs against the daughters of several of the European consuls. Despite all Macdonald's efforts to secure Rosa's release she remained immured until the Dey's death, when the presence of two British warships persuaded his successor not only to free Rosa and another kidnapped girl but to compensate them with an indemnity of 5,000 dollars apiece. A book of memoranda was found amongst the dead Dey's papers containing the following entry: 'Mr Macdonald's daughter, pretty and young, for my harem; the Spanish Consul's daughter, who is ugly, to serve the favourite; I shall have the English Consul's head cut off, and that of the

Spanish Consul too, and all the Consuls shall be killed, if they dare to complain.'[20]

To the statesmen at Aix-la-Chapelle, such incidents may have appeared of very minor importance, but in May 1818 they did at least agree on a document inviting France and England to warn the offenders that unless they mended their ways, the very existence of the Barbary states might be called in question. The French admiral Jurien de la Gravière and the British commodore Freemantle sailed the following year with a joint squadron to present the Powers' ultimatum. The Dey of Algiers rejected it verbally, whilst the Bey of Tunis gave an evasive written reply. The Pasha of Tripoli promised compliance but continued his depredations as before. In 1825, the king of Sardinia succeeded in burning a number of the Pasha's warships in Tripoli harbour, and the following year a French squadron forced him to release three ships belonging to the Papal States and to pay an indemnity. Naples also took reprisals against the recalcitrant city with a heavy bombardment. But when, in 1824, Algerian corsairs had seized a Spanish ship and enslaved its crew, in clear violation of the 1816 undertaking, the punitive bombardment attempted by a British squadron under Sir Henry Neale proved a humiliating failure.

Pierre Deval, the French consul in Algiers, had long been convinced that something far more drastic and fundamental was required. 'It is no use deceiving ourselves,' he had written in 1819,

> We shall never force the Turks of Algiers to yield by means of bombardments, even one hard upon another . . . I think that we must extirpate the evil from the root, and invest Algiers, the soul of this piracy, by land. Once in the hands of the Europeans it would bring down in its ruin the whole system of Algerian piracy and put a curb on the other Barbary states which still persist in not respecting international law.[21]

A crisis in France's relations with Algiers was soon to bring matters to a head. Profitable commercial links had developed between the two countries, but France had remained heavily indebted for the huge quantities of grain imported during the Napoleonic wars. These had been supplied chiefly through the agency of two Jewish merchant families, the Bakri and the Buchnaq. The Dey's finances were in turn largely dependent on the taxes due from the Jews, who protested that they were unable to pay until the French settled their accounts. Dey Husain Pasha blamed the French consul for failing to get his Government to pay up. He also resented the overbearing behaviour of Deval's nephew, who was vice-consul at Bône, and had other grievances. In an angry interview on 29 April 1827 the Dey struck the French consul across the face with his fly-swatter. In former days, France had seen her consuls blown to pieces at the cannon's mouth without being able to exact due vengeance. But now there were powerful pent-up imperialist forces in France waiting for just such a trifling signal to act.

French warships were at once sent to blockade Algiers. They did not however prevent Algerian corsairs continuing to take prizes, French ships included. The merchants of Marseilles clamoured for a lifting of the blockade which was ruining their trade, but when the Dey was invited to send an emissary to Paris to conclude an armistice, he replied by discharging his cannon at the commander-in-chief's flag-ship. The Dey's intransigence strengthened the hands of the war party in France, and even the Marseilles lobby began to believe that its interests would best be served by nothing less than a full-scale occupation of Algiers. The Liberals, however, were against any French involvement in Africa. Polignac, the Prime Minister, held that the problem might be solved by encouraging Muhammad Ali of Egypt, a firm friend of France, to annex the Regencies, but his plans were frustrated by British opposition. The Royalist party saw in a quick victory in Algiers a sure means of increasing the prestige of the monarchy. The decision was taken to invade. In an endeavour to allay the suspicions of the other European powers, the French Government informed them that the expeditionary force was being sent solely for the eradication of slavery and piracy, and that they would be fully consulted when the time came as to the future status of Algiers.[22] Initially, only the occupation of that city and of other key points on the coast was envisaged—basically a strategy of 'limited occupation' which the Spaniards had adopted, with unfortunate results, more than three centuries before.

Algiers capitulated to the French on 5 July 1830, the Dey went into exile, and the janissaries were shipped back to Constantinople. The fall of the city was only the first step in what was to prove the long and difficult task of extending French rule over the whole of the former Regency. The downfall of Algiers, as Deval had foreseen, had immediate repercussions in Tunis and Tripoli which at once proclaimed an end to Christian slavery and corsair activities. They preserved a fictitious independence until becoming respectively, in 1881 and 1911, a French protectorate and an Italian colony. In 1912 the remaining vestiges of Moroccan independence were obliterated by the establishment of French and Spanish protectorates.

The last word goes to a captive who lived through the final phase of Christian slavery and witnessed the downfall of his captors and the disintegration of their system.[23] Simon Friedrich Pfeiffer was a young German surgeon seized by janissaries near Smyrna whilst he was tending some of his Dutch shipmates who had been put ashore ill. He was taken to Algiers on a ship commanded by an English renegade and then set to work as a scullion for the Khaznaji, the official in charge of the state treasury, together with fourteen other slaves of Spanish, Italian, Greek, Dutch and Mexican nationality. He was confined in a rat-infested shed and became a prey to despair and thoughts of suicide. At attempt to escape was frustrated by the treachery of a fellow-slave and only earned him a severe thrashing.

After two years, Pfeiffer was promoted from kitchen service and appointed personal physician to his master, who suffered from obesity. His situation began to improve. He was given a good room and fine clothes and his sufferings were now chiefly from boredom. But these privileges aroused the jealousy of the Khaznaji's nephew who accused him of insulting the Koran, for which he was punished with 250 strokes of the bastinado. In the six weeks Pfeiffer spent recovering from this experience he was cheered by rumours of the deepening crisis between France and Algiers. When a captured French officer was sent him for treatment—the first man he had seen in European clothes for four years—he knew them to be true. Suddenly he was informed by his master that he was free. The Khaznaji's tone was now quite different, and the ex-slave was implored to take responsibility for the many wounded soldiers who were being brought back into the city after a great battle. Pfeiffer claims that he was in fact the only surgeon in Algiers, which was quite without any medical facilities. One of the barracks was quickly turned into a make-shift hospital and 1,500 janissaries and other wounded men were crammed into it. Tents were torn into strips for bandages, and the city's Jewish and Moorish barbers were summoned and told to bring their basins. They proved unwilling and almost useless helpers, who had to be kept to their work by armed sentries posted at the doors.

In the first four hours, Pfeiffer tells us, he managed to bandage 240 wounded men and extracted ninety-five musket balls, and he continued his labours almost at the same pace for a fortnight. In the meantime the French had entered Algiers, and Pfeiffer stood at the door of the hospital to salute the victors, who were amazed to find it in the charge of a young ex-slave. Soon he had nine French doctors sharing the work. The Khaznaji, meanwhile, had sent an urgent message saying that the troops had begun to sack his palace, and 'if they take my treasure, they might as well take my life'. Pfeiffer managed to induce the French general to send a guard which allowed the Khaznaji to load the bulk of his personal fortune onto a ship bound for Constantinople. For these services the Khaznaji swore eternal gratitude which he expressed by bestowing a handful of gold coins to be distributed amongst the wounded. Pfeiffer, for his part, found the recovery of his freedom a sufficient reward, and he was attached to the general's staff until able to return to Europe.

Pfeiffer had witnessed the end of one era and the beginning of another. After the Dey's capitulation, the French commander-in-chief entered the Casbah and found the Khaznaji waiting impassively with the keys of the state treasury. The vaults were unsealed and their glittering contents revealed—sequins minted in Algiers, ingots of gold and silver, chests filled with the currencies of Spain, Mexico, the Ottoman Empire, tribute from the Italian and north European states—a veritable Aladdin's cave crammed with the hoarded spoils of the corsairs' trade. A certificate of transfer was signed and the keys handed over.[24] So great was the accumulated treasure— quite apart from the personal fortunes which the Dey and other high officials were allowed to take with them—that about half of it sufficed to reimburse the French Government for the full cost of the military expedition, whilst the other half disappeared into the pockets of Algeria's new masters.[25] The account opened by the Barbarossa brothers more than three centuries before was at last closed. The corsairs had had their day, and the colonialists lost no time in entering upon their inheritance.

Notes

The following abbreviations are used for the most commonly cited book s

Barnby	H. G. Barnby: *The Prisoners of Algiers—an Account of the Forgotten American-Algerian War 1785–97*, Oxford, 1966.
Bono	S. Bono: *I Corsari Barbareschi*, Turin, 1964.
Braithwaite	J. Braithwaite: *History of the Revolutions in Morocco*, London, 1729.
Braudel	F. Braudel: *The Mediterranean World in the Age of Philip II*, London, 1973.
Brooks	F. Brooks: *Barbarian Cruelty: a True History of the Distressed Condition of Christian Captives under Mully Ishmael*, London, 1693.
Broughton	E. Broughton: *Six Years Residence in Algiers*, London, 1839.
Busnot	P. Busnot: *History of the Reign of Muley Ismael*, London, 1715.
CSP, Dom.	*Calendar of State Papers, Domestic.*
Dan	P. Dan: *Histoire de la Barbarie et de ses Corsaires*, Paris, 1637.
D'Aranda	Emanuel d'Aranda: *Relation de la Captivité à Alger*, Leyden, 1671.
Deslandres	P. Deslandres: *L'Ordre des Trinitaires*, Toulouse, 1903.
Fisher	G. Fisher, *Barbary Legend*, Oxford, 1957.
Foss	John Foss: *Journal of Captivity in Algiers*, Newport, n.d.
García Navarro	M. García Navarro: *Redenciones de Cautivos en Africa 1723–5*, Madrid, 1946.
Gracián	Jerónimo Gracián: *Crónica de Cautiverio y Peregrinación de Anastasio*, Madrid, 1942.
Grammont	H. D. de Grammont: *Histoire d'Alger 1515–1830*, Paris, 1887.
Haedo, *Captividad*	D. de Haedo, *Diálogo de la Captividad*, Valladolid, 1612.
Haedo, *Mártires*	D. de Haedo, *Diálogo de los Mártires*, Valladolid, 1612.
Haedo, *Morabutos*	D. de Haedo, *Diálogo de los Morabutos*, Valladolid, 1612.
Haedo, *Topografía*	D. de Haedo, *Topografía e Historia de Argel*, Valladolid, 1612.
Hakluyt	R. Hakluyt: *Principal Navigations*, London, 1927.
Laugier	Laugier de Tassy: *Histoire d'Alger*, Amsterdam, 1725.
Morgan, *History*	J. Morgan, *History*, London, n.d.

Morgan, *Voyages*   J. Morgan, *Several Voyages to Barbary*, London, n.d.
Mouette   G. Mouette: *Relation de Captivité*, Paris, 1683.
Pellow   T. Pellow: *The Adventures of T. Pellow, Mariner*, London,
                   1890.
Penz   C. Penz: *Les Captifs Français du Maroc au XVII Siècle*,
                   Rabat, 1944.
Playfair   R. L. Playfair: *The Scourge of Christendom*, London, 1884.
Pitts   J. Pitts: *Account of the Religion and Manners of the
                   Mahommetans*, Exeter, 1704.

Chapter 1   Into Bondage

1   Gracián, 79 et seq.
2   D'Aranda, 8–9.
3   Foss, 10–11.

Chapter 2   Moors and Christians

1   P. Levy: *The Social Structure of Islam*, Cambridge, 1957, 221.
2   E. Lévi-Provençal: *Histoire de l'Espagne Musulmane*, Paris, 1953, vol. 3,
    208 et seq.
3   ibid., 105–6.
4   M. Asín Palacios: *Vidas de Santones Andaluces*, 1933, 55–6.
5   F. Simonet: *Historia de los Mozárabes de España*, Madrid, 1897–1903, 633.
6   J. M. de Cossio: *Cautivos de Moros en el Siglo XIII*, in *Al Andalus*, 1942,
    vol. VII, 49–112.
7   Dan, 473–7.
8   J. A. Garí y Siumell: *Redenciones de Cautivos Cristianos*, Barcelona, 1873,
    9 et seq.
9   L. de Marmol: *Historia de los Moriscos*, Madrid, 1797, vol. 2, 397–9.

Chapter 3   The Rise of the Barbary States

1   Hakluyt, vol. 3, 7.
2   J. Caro Baroja: *Los Moriscos del Reino de Granada*, Madrid, 1957, 188.
3   L. de Marmol: *Historia de los Moriscos*, Madrid, 1797, vol. 2, 397–9.
4   Braudel, vol. 2, 1185.

Chapter 4   Corsairs and Captives

1   Dan, 265–6.
2   Dan, 279; Bono, 85–91; Laugier, 262.
3   H. D. de Grammont: *Un Académicien (Jean Foy Vaillant) à Alger* in
    Revue Africaine, vol. XXVI, 1882, 387–96.
4   Braudel, 973.
5   Bono, 159–60, 180–3.

6   Pitts, 73.
7   Broughton, 187.
8   R. Chastelet des Boys: *L'Odyssée*, in *Revue Africaine*, September 1869, vol. XIII, no. 77, 376.
9   Laugier, 278.
10 Haedo, *Topografía*, 38.
11 Pitts, 18.
12 ibid., 47.
13 Foss, 35–6.
14 Haedo, *Topografía*, 38.
15 Laugier, 171–99.
16 Mouette, 284.
17 D'Aranda, 171–5.
18 R. Chastelet des Boys, *Revue Africaine*, January 1869, vol. XII, 29–30.
19 Pitts, 13–14.
20 D'Aranda, 216.
21 ibid., 221–9.
22 Haedo, *Captividad*, 139.
23 Barnby, 120.
24 ibid., 147.
25 *Mémoires de Thédenat*, *Revue Africaine*, 1848, vol. XCII, 143 et seq.
26 J. Blavin: *La Condition de la Vie des Français dans la Régence d'Alger*, Algiers, 1899, 81–7.
27 García Navarro, 339.

Chapter 5   Life in the Bagnios

1   Haedo, *Topografía*, 8.
2   Dan, 282.
3   Bono, 220.
4   Grammont, 268, 274.
5   Pellow, 71.
6   D'Aranda, 237.
7   Broughton, 279.
8   Haedo, *Mártires*, 159.
9   D'Aranda, 266.
10 Broughton, 256.
11 Laugier, 277.
12 Barnby, 250.
13 Laugier, 276.
14 Foss, 19.
15 D'Aranda, 168–175.
16 Foss, 123.
17 D'Aranda, 238.
18 Gracián, 94.
19 M. Fernández de Navarrete: *Vida de Cervantes*, Madrid, 1819, 336–41.

20   Mouette, 116.
21   Penz, 284.
22   Busnot, 145–65.
23   ibid., 104.
24   Mouette, 93–100.
25   Penz, 281.
26   Mouette, 68–70; Pellow, 71; Penz, 288.
27   Mouette, 116.
28   P.-J. Dumont: *Histoire de l'Esclavage en Afrique*, Paris, 1819.
29   ibid., 11.

Chapter 6 Escapes

1   Morgan, *History*, 475.
2   ibid., 275.
3   ibid., 566.
4   ibid., 569.
5   Hakluyt, vol. 3, 38–49.
6   Grammont, 213.
7   ibid., 306.
8   Morgan, *History*, 518.
9   Foss, 31–2.
10   Playfair, 12.
11   Morgan, *History*, 280.
12   Foss, 33.
13   Morgan, *History*, 654–60.
14   T. Lurting: *The Fighting Sailor turn'd Peaceable Christian*, London, 1710, 33–46.
15   Haedo, *Mártires*, 164.
16   Braudel, 874.
17   Morgan, *Voyages*, 58.
18   García Navarro.
19   Haedo, *Mártires*, 185.
20   Bono, 396–403; text of letter in *To Any Christian—Letters from the Saints*, London, 1964, 47–52.
21   Playfair, 59–60; W. Okeley: *Ebenezer, or a Small Monument of Great Mercy*, London, 1675.
22   Grammont, 223.
23   ibid., 263.
24   Playfair, 185.
25   Morgan, *History*, 510.
26   Playfair, 106.
27   Morgan, *Voyages*, 52.
28   Playfair, 180.
29   Mouette, 161–203.
30   Dan, 415–19.

31 Penz, 307.
32 F. Caronni: *Ragguaglio del Viaggio in Berberia*, Milan, 1805, 45.
33 Mouette, 204–7.
34 T. Phelps: *Account of Captivity at Machaness in Barbary*, London, 1685.
35 Brooks, 113.
36 Busnot, 231.
37 ibid., 140.

Chapter 7 Renegades

1 Gracián, 32.
2 Haedo, *Topografía*, 22; *Morabutos*, 193.
3 Braudel, 681.
4 Morgan, *History*, 386, 489, 520, 570.
5 Haedo, *Topografía*, 11, 18.
6 Braudel, 159.
7 Haedo, *Topografía*, 9.
8 Dan, 313–14.
9 Pellow, 30.
10 Bono, 256.
11 Pitts, 142–3.
12 R. Tully: *Narrative of Ten Years Residence at Tripoli*, London, 1816, 233.
13 Mouette, 284–303.
14 Busnot, 152.
15 Braithwaite, 192.
16 Pellow, 54–5.
17 Gracián, 27–8.
18 Brooks, 35.
19 Grammont, 248; Penz, 314.
20 Fisher, 257; Playfair, 121.
21 Pitts, 131.
22 D'Aranda, 260.
23 Bono, 252–3.
24 Gracián, 107.
25 Dan, 347–9.
26 Busnot, 10–11.
27 *Revue Africaine*, November 1868, vol. XII, no. 72, 441.
28 D'Aranda, 292.
29 Dan, 167.
30 L. de Marmol: *Historia de los Moriscos*, Madrid, 1797, vol. 1, 94.
31 Bono, 256–7.
32 Braudel, 759.
33 Bono, 261.
34 Haedo, *Mártires*, 163.
35 Gracián, 95.
36 Miguel de Cervantes: *Don Quixote*, Part I, ch. XIII.

37   Bono, 259–60.
38   R. Coindreau: *Les Corsaires de Salé*, Paris, 1948, 67–9.
39   Braudel, 800.
40   Gracián, 37.
41   Braithwaite, 180.
42   Broughton, 292.
43   *CSP, Dom., 1607–10*, 49, 54, 140, 226.
44   Braithwaite, 185–6.
45   Pellow, 32.
46   Bono, 253.
47   Morgan, *History*, 532.

Chapter 8   Ransoms

1   D'Aranda, 387.
2   Bono, 275.
3   ibid., 273–4.
4   ibid., 274–5.
5   Mouette, 308–14.
6   Gracián, 168.
7   Bono, 325–6.
8   J. Blavin: *La Condition de la Vie des Français dans la Régence d'Alger*, Algiers, 1899, 64.
9   Mouette, 326.
10   Gracián, 110–15.
11   Bono, 284–309.
12   Deslandres, vol. I, 357 et seq.
13   G. Aranda: *Vida de Fernando de Contreras*, Seville, 1692, 272 et seq.
14   Dan, 481.
15   Deslandres, vol. I, 331.
16   ibid., 436.
17   J. A. Garí y Siumell: *Historia de las Redenciones*, Cadiz, 1873; J. B. Herrada Armijo: *El Voto de Redención en la Orden de la Merced*, Santiago de Chile, 1951, 142–8.
18   Deslandres, vol. I, 331.
19   J. A. Garí y Siumell: *Historia de las Redenciones*, Cadiz, 1873, 366.
20   *Revue Africaine*, 1869, vol. XIII, 383.
21   Haedo, *Topografía*, 24.
22   Barnby, 217.
23   Laugier, 281.
24   Deslandres, vol. I, 377 et seq.
25   D'Aranda, 96.
26   Bono, 280–1.
27   Examples in Bono, 282 and Dan, 446.
28   Deslandres, vol. I, 394.

29 C. Verlinden: *L'Esclavage dans l'Europe Mediévale—Peninsule Iberique*, 1955, 542.
30 Haedo, *Captividad*, 145.
31 Dan, 501–4; Calixte: *Les Captifs Illustres*, 1892, 241.
32 Calixte: *Les Captifs Illustres*, 1892, 316; Deslandres, vol. I, 403–5.
33 García Navarro.
34 Barnby, 46.
35 Morgan, *Voyages*, 70.
36 Braithwaite, 199–200.
37 Dan, 506–13.
38 J. Coppin: *Le Bouclier de l'Europe*, Lyon, 1686, 406–7.
39 García Navarro, 303.
40 Bono, 245–6.
41 J.-B. de la Faye: *Etat des Royaumes de Barbarie*, The Hague, 1704, 45–6.
42 Dan, 434–5.
43 D'Aranda, 186, 194.
44 Haedo, *Topografía*, 36.
45 Dan, 506.
46 ibid., 436.
47 J. Blavin: *La Condition de la Vie des Français dans la Régence d'Alger*, Algiers, 1899, 39.
48 J. B. S. Orse: *Alger pendant 100 Ans*, Paris, 1865, 70.
49 Grammont 197.

Chapter 9 The English Slaves

1   *CSP, Dom., 1547–80*, 295.
2   Hakluyt, vol. 3, 131.
3   ibid., 155–6.
4   ibid., 117–19.
5   ibid., 120.
6   *The Miserable Captivity of Richard Hasleton* in C. R. Beazeley, *Voyages and Travels*, London, 1902, vol. 2, 151–80.
7   Thomas Saunders: *The Unfortunate Voyage of the 'Jesus' to Tripoli* in Hakluyt, vol. 3, 139–55.
8   ibid., 153–5.
9   ibid., 367–8.
10 ibid., 358.
11 Playfair, 32–3.
12 P. Earl: *Corsairs of Malta and Barbary*, London, 1970, 50.
13 Playfair, 34.
14 Morgan, *History*, 629–31.
15 ibid., 632–7.
16 *CSP, Dom., 1623–5*, 287.
17 Playfair, 46–7.
18 ibid., 50–62.

19   D'Aranda, 237.
20   Devereux Spratt: *Autobiography*, London, 1886.
21   W. Okeley: *Ebenezer, or a Small Monument of Great Mercy*, London, 1675, 24.
22   J. Coppin: *Le Bouclier de l'Europe*, Lyon, 1686, 407–8.
23   Fisher, 202; *CSP, Dom.*, *1628–9*, 356.
24   Fisher, 206.
25   Playfair, 55.
26   *CSP, Dom.*, *1640*, 321.
27   ibid., 450.
28   *CSP, Dom.*, *1640–1*, 134.
29   Playfair, 63–70.
30   ibid., 83–7
31   Fisher, 264.
32   Playfair, 128–30.
33   Fisher, 253.
34   Text in Morgan, *History*, 681 et seq.
35   Grammont, 247.
36   Fisher, 281.
37   Playfair, 176, 217, 242.
38   Hakluyt, vol. 4, 156.
39   C. J. Julien: *History of North Africa*, London, 1970, 235.
40   *CSP, Dom.*, *1624–6*, 79, 414, 516.
41   *CSP, Dom.*, *1626*, 257.
42   ibid., 339.
43   *CSP, Dom.*, *1625*, 85.
44   *CSP, Dom.*, *1631–3*, 219.
45   *CSP, Dom.*, *1626*, 458; Fisher, 322.
46   *CSP, Dom.*, *1626*, 480.
47   *CSP, Dom.*, *1633–4*, 215–16.
48   *CSP, Dom.*, *1635*, 476.
49   *CSP, Dom.*, *1635–6*, 15.
50   *CSP, Dom.*, *1635*, 69.
51   *CSP, Dom.*, *1637*, 87, 431.
52   ibid., 7.
53   Brooks, 23.
54   Pellow, 103.
55   Brooks, 58; T. Osborne: *Collection of Voyages*, London, 1745, vol. 2, 492–7.
56   Braithwaite, 352–3.

Chapter *10*   From Corsairs to Colonialists

1   A. F. Nettement: *Histoire de la Conquête de l'Alger*, Paris, 1856, 84.
2   T. Troughton: *Barbarian Cruelty; Narrative of the Sufferings of the British Captives Belonging to the 'Inspector' Privateer*, London, 1751.

3   Playfair, 206–7.
4   ibid., 209–12.
5   ibid., 181.
6   ibid., 186.
7   ibid., 191–2.
8   R. W. Irwin: *The Diplomatic Relations of the United States with the Barbary Powers, 1776–1816*, N. Carolina Press, 1931, 80–1.
9   Barnby, 296–7.
10 Playfair, 243–4.
11 Bono, 326 et seq.
12 J. M. Abun-Nasr: *History of the Maghrib*, Cambridge, 1971, 198–200.
13 F. Pananti: *Narrative of Residence in Algiers*, London, 1818.
14 ibid., 412 et seq.
15 E. Howard: *Memoirs of Sir Sidney Smith*, London, 1839, vol. 2, 194 et seq.
16 P.-J. Dumont: *Histoire de l'Esclavage en Afrique*, Paris, 1819, 31.
17 A. Salame: *Narrative of the Expedition to Algiers*, London, 1819, 22–3.
18 ibid., 101.
19 ibid., 109.
20 Playfair, 282–4.
21 F. Charles-Roux: *France et l'Afrique du Nord avant 1830*, Paris, 1932, 523.
22 A. F. Nettement: *Histoire de la Conquête de l'Alger*, Paris, 1856, 266–8.
23 S. F. Pfeiffer: *Reisen und Gefangenschaft*, Giessen, 1832.
24 A. F. Nettement: *Histoire de la Conquête de l'Alger*, Paris, 1856, 442–4.
25 J. M. Abun-Nasr: *History of the Maghrib*, Cambridge, 1971, 238.

Index